THE EVOLUTION
OF CAPITALISM

THE EVOLUTION
OF CAPITALISM

Advisory Editor
LEONARD SILK
Editorial Board,
The New York Times

Research Associate
MARK SILK

CATHOLICISM, PROTESTANTISM AND CAPITALISM

BY

AMINTORE FANFANI

ARNO PRESS

A NEW YORK TIMES COMPANY

New York • 1972

Reprint Edition 1972 by Arno Press Inc.

Reprinted by permission of Sheed and Ward Ltd.

Reprinted from a copy in
The University of Illinois Library

The Evolution of Capitalism
ISBN for complete set: 0-405-04110-1
See last pages of this volume for titles.

Manufactured in the United States of America

- - - - - - - - - - - -

Library of Congress Cataloging in Publication Data

Fanfani, Amintore.
    Catholicism, Protestantism and capitalism.

    (The Evolution of capitalism)
    Reprint of the 1935 ed.
    Translation of Cattolicesimo e Protestantesimo nella
formazione storica del capitalismo.
    Includes bibliographical references.
    1. Capitalism. 2. Protestantism. 3. Church
and social problems--Catholic Church. 4. Social
ethics. I. Title. II. Series.
HB501.F32 1972   330.12'2   78-38251
ISBN 0-405-04119-5

CATHOLICISM, PROTESTANTISM
AND
CAPITALISM

CATHOLICISM, PROTESTANTISM AND CAPITALISM

BY

AMINTORE FANFANI

Lecturer in Economic History
in the
University of the Sacred Heart, Milan

LONDON
SHEED & WARD
1935

THIS TRANSLATION OF
CATTOLICESIMO E PROTESTANTESIMO NELLA
FORMAZIONE STORICA DEL CAPITALISMO
(COPYRIGHT: SOCIETÀ EDITRICE " VITA E PENSIERO ")
WAS FIRST PUBLISHED IN
MAY 1935
BY SHEED AND WARD
FROM 31 PATERNOSTER ROW
LONDON E.C.4

PRINTED BY THE WHITEFRIARS PRESS LTD.
LONDON AND TONBRIDGE

CONTENTS

V

CATHOLICISM, PROTESTANTISM AND CAPITALISM

CHAPTER I

THE TERMS OF THE PROBLEM

1. Religion and our problem. 2. The idea of capitalism.
3. Lines of treatment.

1. THE relations between religion and capitalism are
vague and hard to determine if by capitalism we mean
merely a complexus of technical methods and institutions, facilitating and regulating in a certain definite
manner the production, circulation, and distribution of
wealth in recent times and to a large extent to-day.[1]

---

[1] We say "to a large extent to-day," because it is well known that many
speak of a decline of the capitalistic system beginning in the period immediately
before the war.

See in this connection: G. Del Vecchio, "Il problema della stabilità del
sistema economico capitalistico" in *Economia*, 1925; G. Schumpeter,
"The Instability of Capitalism" in *The Economic Journal*, 1928; Gerhardt,
"Ende des Kapitalismus ?" in *Zeitwende*, 1928; C. Muhs, "Die Chance
des Kapitalismus" in *Weltwirtschaftliches Archiv*, 1930; A. Weber, *Ende
des Kapitalismus?*, Munich, Hüber, 1930; R. Giraud, *Vers une internationale
économique*, Paris, Valois, 1931; M. Kellersohn, *Contre un cataclysme économique*, Paris, Stock, 1931; Spengler, *Der Mensch und die Technik*, Munich,
1931 (Eng. tr., *Man and Technics*, London, 1932); F. Vito, "Il problema
della stabilità del capitalismo nella letteratura" in *Rivista Internazionale di
Scienze Sociali*, September, 1931; Rev. L. Watt, S.J., *The Future of Capitalism*,
The Catholic Social Guild, 1931; F. Fried, *Das Ende des Kapitalismus*,
1932; P. Lucius, *Faillite du capitalisme?*, Paris, Payot, 1932; L. Romier,
La crise du capitalisme, Pt. II of *Problèmes économiques de l'heure présente*,
Montreal, Lévesque, 1932; W. Sombart, *Die Zukunft des Kapitalismus*,

With this conception of capitalism, research into the problem would be possible indeed, but fraught with grave difficulties, and our conclusions would be meagre. At the most, we should probably find that religion had had a very indirect influence on the *forms* of capitalism.

Whereas, if capitalism is envisaged instead as a complete social system, the question of its relations with religion acquires a far greater significance.

These brief reflections, the outcome of prolonged meditation, justify us from the start in our attempt to reach an accurate formulation of the terms of the problem. If it is to be satisfactorily solved, it must be clearly presented. It is therefore necessary for us to determine exactly between what aspects of religion and what aspects of capitalism we must seek for relation.

Religion may influence life in general, and economic life in particular, in one of two ways—either as a doctrinal system or as an organization. These two aspects of religion are frequently confused. Historians of the acumen of Sée argue that it is untrue to say that Catholicism has not favoured the capitalistic spirit, since, on the contrary, the Papacy contributed to its establishment.[1] Others hold that the Catholic religion encouraged capitalism, on the grounds that the mediæval Popes

Berlin, Bucholz, 1932 ; B. S. Chlepner, " L'avenir du capitalisme " in *Revue de l'Institut de Sociologie*, 1933 ; Pirou, Sombart, Durbin, Patterson, Spirito, *La crisi del capitalismo*, Florence, Sansoni, 1933 ; A. Fanfani, " Declino del capitalismo e significato del corporativismo " in *Giornale degli Economisti*, 1934.

[1] H. Sée, review of the author's " Le origini dello spirito capitalistico in Italia " in *The Economic History Review*, vol. IV, No. 2, April, 1933, p. 249.

protected certain bankers, or encouraged their accumulation of wealth by entrusting them with the collection of tithes in certain districts. The two aspects are distinct and should be treated as such. The relations between capitalism and the Catholic religion must not be confused with the relations between capitalism and the Catholic Church as an organization.

In spite of this unconscious confusion, most of the historians who have dealt at all directly with the problem have considered religion more as a system of morals than as ecclesiastical organization. A typical example of this is provided by Max Weber, whose position is clear from the very title of his work: *Die protestantische Ethik und der Geist des Kapitalismus* (Protestant ethics and the spirit of capitalism). It goes without saying that this attitude does not in the least imply neglect of the mystical, still less of the theological content of religion. Such dissociation would be impossible, for moral doctrine is bound up with, or, better, founded on, the theological doctrine, and if, for scientific convenience, it may be considered apart, in reality it is only another aspect of the same fact; it is a system of corollaries, deduced from a system of postulates. Theology provides the principles, morals their application, and the two are indissolubly linked. If in estimating the relations between religion and capitalism it is convenient to consider the moral aspect involved without explicit reference to underlying theology, the conclusions reached will be none the less valid. As we have explained, full account is taken of religion even when only its moral implications are under consideration.

It is our intention to investigate the relations between Catholicism and Protestantism on the one hand, and the development of capitalism on the other.[1] Since capitalism is definitely an economic and social phenomenon, we shall confine our research to the influence of the religions we have mentioned on man's outlook not on the problems of life as a whole but on problems of an economic and social character. And since ecclesiastical organizations as such have also had relations with capitalism, we shall warn our readers when we are referring to the organization as distinct from the ideology of religion. Thus, while avoiding the confusion of issues that we have criticized in other writers, we shall

---

[1] The problem that we are considering is not a new one. It was early formulated by scholars who sought in religious factors an explanation of the strange and almost sudden displacement of the centre of economic activity from Southern and Catholic Europe to North-Western and Protestant Europe, from the sixteenth century onwards. This problem was exploited for apologetic purposes by nineteenth-century controversialists. It lent itself both to the fervent admirers and implacable critics of the capitalist system, who, according to their respective standpoints, claimed for their religion the credit of having either encouraged or opposed the development of capitalism. At the end of the nineteenth and beginning of the twentieth century, it became a sociological problem that had necessarily to be faced by anyone desirous of explaining the progress of the world and of modern civilization.

There is no need to enumerate the authors who have studied this question in recent times, since this has been done in a bibliographical study, " Riforma e capitalismo moderno nella recente letteratura " in *Rivista Internazionale di Scienze Sociali*, July, 1930. We wish, however, to mention a name that is there omitted, William Temple, who was one of the first to relate the economic life of Protestant countries to religion in his essay, *Observations upon the United Provinces of the Netherlands*, recently reprinted (Cambridge, Cambridge Press, 1932) ; and also the quite recent essay by H. M. Robertson, *The Rise of Economic Individualism* (Cambridge University Press, 1933), in which the author definitely criticizes the religious interpretation of the development of the capitalistic spirit.

overlook no aspect, however insignificant, of the possible relations, direct and indirect, between Catholicism, Protestantism and capitalism.

2. In defining the terms of the problem, we have dealt with religion; it now remains for us to define "capitalism."

Many attempts have been made to reduce this historical phenomenon to certain of its characteristic features. Each student of the question has taken one particular conception, with the result that widely different conclusions have been reached.

Recently, Vito, the Italian economist, held that capitalism could be identified with " the economic system characterized by (a) free choice of activity on the part of economic agents ; (b) private ownership of the means of production; (c) competition." [1] Other writers, earlier and more recent, identified capitalism with the prevalence of big industry. Others again see its distinguishing feature as circulating capital. Yet another author considers its chief characteristic to be the relative predominance of capital over labour.[2] Von Zwiedineck-Südenhorst [3] expresses capitalism in function of capital, whereas Labriola holds contrary

---

[1] F. Vito, *Il problema della stabilità*.
[2] E. Wagemann, *Struktur und Rhythmus der Weltwirtschaft*, Berlin, 1931, pp. 30–39.
[3] O. Von Zwiedineck-Südenhorst, " Kapital und Kapitalismus " in *Schmollers Jahrbuch*, 54th year, 1930, p. 1059. Also " Was macht ein Zeitalter kapitalistisch ? " in *Zeitschrift für die ges. Staatswissenschaft*, 90 B., 1931, pp. 483–524.

views.[1] In general, the economists prefer definitions that are strictly concerned with economic means, and believe, albeit mistakenly, that the historian would do well to confine his attention to these. Whereas the historian, by definition, must take many factors into account that the economist has so far found it convenient to leave aside. The sociologists eschew economic definitions, and show a particular affection for those of wider scope, in which the economic factor is merely a component part.[2] It was precisely such sociologists as Max Weber, whose work is of high value, or Werner Sombart, whose competence, though disputed, is undeniable, who arrived at an idea of capitalism that was less economic and more sociological than that commonly accepted by the economists.[3] Even historians, who in general have no love for sociology,[4] incline towards a broad conception of capitalism, rather than towards one restricted and mainly determined by technical means. One of the most noted of such historians, R. H. Tawney, presents the original view that capitalism is rather a mode of life, determined by a spiritual orientation, than a system of

---

[1] A. Labriola, *Capitalismo*, Naples, 1926, pp. 329 sq.

[2] For the significations of the term " capitalism " among the Germans, see P. Passow, *Kapitalismus*, Jena, Fischer, 1926.

[3] See especially M. Weber, " Die protestantische Ethik und der Geist des Kapitalismus " in *Archiv für Sozialwissenschaft und Sozialpolitik*, vol. XX-XXI, 1904–5, Eng. tr. *The Protestant Ethic and the Rise of Capitalism*, London, 1928 ; W. Sombart, *Der Moderne Kapitalismus*, Munich, Duncker, various editions, 1902–24 ; *Der Bourgeois*, Munich, Duncker, 1913, Eng. tr. *The Quintessence of Capitalism*, London, 1916.

[4] Tawney in " The Study of Economic History " (in *Economica*, February, 1933) maintains the necessity of bringing a sociological outlook to bear on research in economic history.

organizing labour.[1]   At bottom, this is the opinion of
many who speak of capitalism and mean now a system
in which capital is predominant, now a system characterized by free labour, and now a system in which
competition is unbridled, credit expands, banks prosper,
big industry assumes gigantic dimensions, and the world
market becomes one.   For such authors the existence
of capitalism depends on the scale of the means of production ; on the range of the means for circulating
wealth ; on the elaboration of tools and plant.   It may
justly be objected that if such criteria are accepted as
the hall-mark of capitalism, the capitalist system has no
original features and no novelty.   Indeed, well-meaning
men have not failed to note that, at bottom, the capitalism that others believed to have made a first tentative appearance in the fifteenth century,[2] flourished in
Florence and in Italy generally in the fourteenth century.[3]
Yet others have added that it could be found in the
Flemish and French cities about the same period,[4] and

[1] R. H. Tawney, *Religion and the Rise of Capitalism*, London, 2nd ed.,
1929.
[2] There was a time when Sombart accepted this date.   It is known that
Marx (*Das Kapital*, Bk. I, Chap. XXVII) dates the capitalistic era from the
sixteenth century, but declares the first appearances of capitalistic production
to have taken place in the fourteenth and fifteenth centuries.   This is Lipson's
view in regard to England (*The Economic History of England, The Middle
Age*, 5th ed., London, Black, 1929).
[3] Innumerable works have been written on this subject.   See the bibliography in our earlier publication.
[4] H. Pirenne, *Les périodes de l'histoire sociale du capitalisme*, Brussels, 1922 ;
Les Villes au moyen age, Brussels, various editions, 1927 (Eng. tr. *Mediæval
Cities*, Princetown, at the University Press, 1925) ; " Les marchands batteurs
de Dinant au XIV et au XV siècle " in *Vierteljahrschrift für Sozial- und
Wirtschaftsgeschichte*, 1904.   Also " Un grand commerce d'exportation au
moyen age : les vins de France " in *Annales d'histoire économique et sociale*,
1933, p. 239.

as early as the eleventh century in Venice.[1] An attempt to trace back the origins of capitalism—given his interpretation of the term—to a far earlier period was made by Slonimski,[2] who held that " the separation between the workers and the means of production, which forms the foundation and essence of capitalism, is a fact of economic life to be found in earliest antiquity ; to associate this fact with recent times, which begin with the sixteenth century, is to know nothing of history." (Here Slonimski is criticizing Marx.) Salvioli [3] is more moderate when, leaping back a thousand years further than Strieder and Pirenne, but stopping short a good deal before Slonimski, he finds capitalism in the time of the Cæsars ; this he qualifies as " ancient," to distinguish it from that of our time.

Is this, then, the originality of the capitalist system ? Is this its novelty ? Has it always existed ? Has there been simply a quantitative variation in the magnitude of the means it employs and the range of its institutions ?

To begin with, as against those who are too eager to find capitalism in every age, we must deny any real and substantial identity in the means, institutions, and economic instruments of various epochs. Then, and this is still more important, we must deny that those who identify the capitalist system with its means, institutions,

---

[1] R. Heynen, *Zur Entstehung des Kapitalismus in Venedig*, Stuttgart, 1905, p. 123.
[2] M. Slonimski, *Versuch einer Kritik der K. Marx'schen ökonomischen Theorien*, Berlin, 1899, p. 13.
[3] G. Salvioli, *Il capitalismo antico*, Bari, 1929.

and economic forms, without considering its ends, have hit the mark. They have not discovered what is often called the essence of capitalism. Capitalism is a complex phenomenon, and one that is not purely economic. It is wholly original, and was perhaps unknown to any age but that which followed the thirteenth or fourteenth centuries. It is a phenomenon that cannot be reduced to one of its innumerable aspects without travesty. Nor is any scientific purpose served by the assumption of a concept of capitalism that varies with the point of view from which it is envisaged. As against Schlösinger's [1] proposal to consider capitalism as severally economic, politico-social, ethico-psychological, and sociological, we must urge that this subdivision of a phenomenon into its partial aspects can be surmounted if, instead of concentrating on the incidental manifestations of capitalism, we seek the essential core of the phenomenon. Only by isolating its essential principle can we gain an idea of its nature, appraise its originality, and realize its distinctive features. And once we have grasped the essence, we shall be able to judge how many of the various phenomena of modern times are bound up with the more comprehensive phenomenon of capitalism, for we shall find that such phenomena either came into being as soon as capitalism appeared, or else were modified by its appearance. And since capitalism is above all an economic mode of life as led by man and by society,

---

[1] A. Schlösinger, " Der Begriff Kapitalismus " in *Soziale Revue*, March, 1933.

we may be led to conclude that it is not absurd to speak of a capitalist spirit. When once we have identified this spirit, so as to find a rational explanation of why society and man at a given period should have lived, that is, existed and acted, in a given manner, we shall then be able to explain why, at a given period, man and society, in order to act and to attain given ends, should have used such and such methods, such and such institutions. In this sense and for this reason we may truly say that the capitalist spirit is the essence of capitalism, in that it holds its secret, conditions and explains it. It is this spirit that, governing impulses and resolutions to action, determines the creation of new means and new institutions or the modification of those already in existence.[1]

Having thus determined what is the essential aspect of capitalism that we must consider in order to investigate the influence of the Christian religion, Catholic and Protestant, on its development, we may proceed to the solution of the problem.

---

[1] Weber, in his *Protestant Ethic* (Chap. I, art. 2) writes : " Enquiry into the forces that encouraged the expansion of modern capitalism is not, at any rate primarily, an enquiry into the source of the monetary reserves to be utilized as capital, but, above all, an enquiry into the development of the capitalistic spirit. Where this spirit reveals itself and seeks realization, it procures monetary capital as means for its action, but the reverse does not hold good."

Recently there have been other instances of the modern tendency to explain economic and social facts in moral terms. Roerig insists on the spiritual causes of " the historical destiny of the Hanseatic League." " Les raisons intellectuelles d'une suprématie commerciale : la Hanse " in *Annales d'histoire economique et sociale*, 15th October, 1930, No. 8. Mornet too has devoted a large volume to a detailed analysis of the intellectual origins of the French Revolution (*Les origines intellectuelles de la Révolution Française*, Paris, Colin, 1933).

3. It should now be easy to understand the method we shall adopt.

We shall take into consideration—even where we do not explicitly say so—all the research that has been made into the economic activities of men at different periods ; we shall make use also of the detailed analysis we ourselves made in an earlier work on the origins of the capitalistic spirit in Italy, and which might almost serve as introduction to the present volume ; and we shall seek, first of all, to define what is meant by the capitalist spirit, how it reveals itself, and what are its chief features. The various objections brought forward against our idea of a capitalist spirit, as presented in the book we have mentioned,[1] have not led us to abandon it. On the contrary, presented with greater precision, it forms the basis of the present work. For we are convinced that, as stated elsewhere,[2] nothing else has that essential quality that permits of the identification of the capitalist system wherever and whenever it may occur. If in this, as in our earlier work, we have achieved anything tangible, we do not hesitate to say that it is the fruit of our effort to determine ever more precisely one of the fundamental characteristics of capitalism. We shall be able to see what has been the influence of this spirit in promoting the transformation of the instruments of economic life—bearing in mind that if practical condi-

[1] Reviews by L. Einaudi, in *La Riforma Sociale*, 1933 ; R. Gonnard, in *Revue d'Economie Politique*, 1933 ; G. Luzzatto, in *Nuova Rivista Storica*, 1933 ; H. Sée, in *The Economic History Review*, 1933 ; F. Chessa, in *Annali di Statistica e di Economia*, vol. II, 1934.

[2] *Declino del capitalismo*, op. cit.

tions tended to bring about such a transformation, it would not have taken place as it did without the presence of a particular disposition in the men concerned. We shall then proceed to investigate in what way the predominance of a capitalistic mentality has transformed public institutions.

Having thus presented a descriptive synthesis of the course of economic and social history under the impulse of the capitalist spirit, we shall pass on to the second stage of our study. To this end we shall reconstruct the economic ethic of Catholicism and examine first its relations with the capitalist ethic, then its influence on the creation of capitalistic institutions and means, ascertaining both the influence exerted directly upon such institutions and means and that exerted on the spirit that produced them. We shall then do the same in regard to Protestantism, though not before devoting a chapter to deciding whether the capitalist spirit had or had not already developed when Protestantism arose. In this same chapter we shall refer briefly to those factors which, independently of religion, may have had an influence on either the spirit or the institutions of capitalism, so that it may be clear that, though we are concentrating on the influence of religious factors on the capitalist phenomenon, we are far from thinking that there were no others.

Since, as we have already pointed out, not only religion as an ethical code, but also religion as an organization and in the persons of its exponents, had relations with capitalism, we shall not fail to make brief reference to such relations, in order to make our conclusions clearer.

In our concluding section we shall consider the problem of the causes of the greater development of capitalism in Protestant as compared with Catholic countries; we shall thus gain a still clearer idea of the part played by the religious factor.

CHAPTER II

1. THE enquiry into the origins of modern capitalism raised the problem of the distinguishing features of capitalism. Many investigators, having turned their attention to this premise to their main problem, ended by concluding that the essential characteristic, or rather the central force that has determined the triumph of the capitalist system in modern civilization, is the capitalist spirit. This conclusion changed the problem of the origins of capitalism into that of the nature and origins of its spirit. It is this spirit that, in the words chosen as title for the English translation of Sombart's *Der Bourgeois*, is " The Quintessence of Capitalism."

Having thus, by successive steps, narrowed down the field of research to its primordial object, the Germans were among the first to devote themselves to its elucidation, using their own methodical procedure. They linked the origins of the capitalist spirit to the religious conception inspiring the peoples among whom capitalism is to-day in vogue.

14

Max Weber gave the Calvinistic current of Protestantism the credit of introducing the idea of vocation, which to-day, though it has lost the religious inspiration of other days, is still the mainspring of modern capitalism.[1]

Ernst Tröltsch attributes an important part to neo-Protestantism in the development of the modern economic spirit, and, while admitting the part played by Humanism and the anabaptist sects in its formation, he gives the chief credit to Calvinism.[2]

In opposition to these two, the chief of those who maintain the preponderant influence of the Reformation, we find, among others, von Below [3] and Brentano,[4] who assert the importance of spiritual influences prior to Protestantism, and Robertson,[5] who confutes Weber's theory.

Sombart [6] gives priority not to the Reformers, but to the Jews, while he attributes their special aptitude for

---

[1] M. Weber, *Die prot. Ethik*, loc. cit. (Eng. tr., pp. 43–44), and " Die protestantischen Sekten und der Geist des Kapitalismus " in *Gesammelte Aufsätze zur Religionssoziologie*, vol. I, Tübingen, 1920. For a criticism of Weber's position, see Chap. VII of the present work.

[2] E. Tröltsch, *Die Bedeutung des Protestantismus für die Entstehung der modernen Welt*, Munich, 1911 (Eng. tr. *Protestantism and Progress*, London, 1930), and *Die Soziallehren der christlichen Kirchen und Gruppen*, Tübingen, 1912 (Eng. tr. *The Social Teaching of the Christian Churches*, London, 1931).

[3] G. Von Below, *Probleme der Wirtschaftsgeschichte*, Tübingen, 1926, Chap. II, Sec. 2.

[4] L. Brentano, " Puritanismus und Kapitalismus " and " Die Anfänge des modernen Kapitalismus " in *Der wirtschaftende Mensch in der Geschichte*, Leipzig, 1923.

[5] H. M. Robertson, *The Rise of Economic Individualism*. For the position of this writer, see Chap. VII, sec. 3, of the present work.

[6] W. Sombart, *Der moderne Kapitalismus*, Leipzig, 1902–3, and *Die Juden und das Wirtschaftsleben*, Leipzig, 1911 (Eng. tr. *The Jews and Modern Capitalism*, London, 1913).

business to racial factors. His is a poor, ingenuous theory, which was in a certain fashion anticipated by L. B. Alberti.[1] It is weak, moreover, for the additional reason that it fails to explain the passing of economic predominance from races that were once masters of commerce to other races that at one time showed no disposition for it.

If Weber and Tröltsch have not lacked critics, Sombart brought a veritable hornets' nest about his ears. His work, as Luzzatto remarked, had the fortune to arouse "a frenzy of critical and polemical writings, research and complementary studies."[2]

Cunningham, Tawney, Halbwachs, Sée, Rougier, Brey, Wünsch, Batault, Lilley, Sommerville, Levy, Binycon, O'Brien, Hauser, Strieder, Kraus, Fisher, Lanfenburger,[3] to quote only a few names, arranged at random, have also

[1] L. B. Alberti, *I primi tre libri della famiglia*, Florence, 1911, lib. I, pp. 71–72.

[2] G. Luzzatto, Preface to the Italian translation of Sombart's *Modern Capitalism* (Florence, 1925, p. 6).

[3] W. Cunningham, *Christianity and Economic Science*, London, 1911.

Tawney, "Religion and Business" in *The Hibbert Journal*, 1922, and *Religion and the Rise of Capitalism*; M. Halbwachs, "Les origines puritaines du capitalisme moderne" in *Revue d'Histoire et de Philosophie Religieuses*, March-April, 1925; H. Sée, *Les origines du capitalisme moderne*, Paris, 1926.

L. Rougier, "La réforme et le capitalisme moderne" in *Revue de Paris*, 15th October, 1928; B. Brey, *Hochscholastik und Geist des Kapitalismus*, Munich, 1927; G. Wünsch, *Evangelische Wirtschaftsethik*, Tübingen, 1927; G. Batault, "Judaisme et puritanisme" in *Revue Universelle*, I, 4, 1921; H. Sommerville, "The Protestant Parentage of Capitalism" in *The Christian Democrat*, No. 2, 1930; H. Levy, *Der Wirtschaftsliberalismus in England*, 2, Jena, 1928; G. Clive Binycon, "Religion and the Rise of Capitalism" in *Stockholm*, No. 2, 1930; G. O'Brien, *An Essay on the Economic Effects of the Reformation*, London, 1923; H. Hauser, *Les Débuts du capitalisme*, Paris, 1927.

J. B. Kraus, *Scholastik, Puritanismus und Kapitalismus*, Munich, 1930; J. Strieder, *Studien* and "Origin and Evolution of Early European Capitalism" in *The Journal of Economic and Business History*, vol. II, No. 1,

studied the question. Some, like Tawney, Kraus, and Levy, have thrown fresh light upon it. Brey has defined its scope. O'Brien has made it clearer. While others, like Lilley, have repeated what is already known, for purposes that are more or less secretly apologetic.[1]

When so much has been written, it is impossible to say in a few words who is right and who is wrong in attributing to this or that religious conception full responsibility for the capitalist spirit. For the capitalist spirit sought by Weber is not the same as that sought by Sombart, or that which Pirenne recently discovered to have inspired St. Godric, whose actions, before his conversion, were wholly devoted to the pursuit of gain, so much so, continues the Belgian historian, that " one clearly recognizes in him that famous capitalist spirit which some would have us believe did not appear till the Renaissance." [2]

All this brings us back to our starting-point, to where we asked ourselves : what is the capitalist spirit ? And to make this question more comprehensible and the problem clearer, we must frame it thus : what is the economic spirit informing modern man when he attends to business ? When we have found an accurate answer

1929 ; H. A. L. Fisher, " The Ethics of Capitalism " in *Monthly Review of Lloyds Bank*, No. 38, April, 1933 ; H. Lanfenburger, "Religion und Wirtschaft im Elsass," in *Archiv. für Soxialwissenschaft und Soxialpolitik*, 1930, pp. 316 sq.

The authors of all these works either put forward a personal view of the " capitalist spirit " or accept (implicitly or explicitly) some conception already formulated by others, though in each case modifying it in some respect.

[1] For the justification of these assertions, cf. A. Fanfani, *Riforma e capitalismo moderno nella recente letteratura*.

[2] H. Pirenne, *Les villes du Moyen Age*, p. 105 (Eng. tr., p. 122).

to this question, we shall be able to pass on to a second, the most important of all for the purposes of the present work : How has religion, Catholic and Protestant, affected the development of this capitalist spirit ?

In order to avoid a number of objections, otherwise inevitable, it must not be forgotten that the manifestation of a certain economic spirit in an exceptional individual is a very different thing from the manifestation of the same spirit in a group of men who have control of social life and can compel it to move in accordance with the spirit with which they are informed. It must always be remembered that, in our investigations, we are concerned with a social force, not an individual passion.[1] So long as the capitalist spirit remains the " sin " of the individual, it is not a force that will organize the world. It is only when it becomes the ideal of successive generations that it can concern us. If this is remembered—and it has often been overlooked—it will save many from announcing to the world that they have discovered the capitalist spirit (as understood by Weber, for example) in some Tom of the fourth century, or a Dick of the twelfth.

The appearance of the capitalist spirit is a phenomenon that can be taken into consideration only from the moment that it begins its uninterrupted course to the moment that it seems on the verge of extinction. We can put it still more strongly. The manifestations of this spirit

[1] Luzzatto, *Storia economica, L'età moderna*, Padua, 1934, p. 67. It is not a question of discovering this or that mentality, but of " determining, if possible, which was the predominant mentality that exercised a real influence at a given period."

18

are of real importance only when the classes that it informs have become the holders of power, and are in a position to give society the imprint that stamps it as capitalist.

Thus isolated individuals who in a given period may be informed by a capitalistic spirit, but who are not linked by any continuity to individuals informed by that spirit in succeeding periods, cannot be taken into consideration, save, up to a point, as exceptional fore-runners of a phenomenon yet to come into being, when causes and circumstances are such as to ensure its prolonged and progressive development in space and time. Recently Lemoine [1] very appositely pointed out that capitalism does not exist till it constitutes an " entire régime." The well-known and remarkable episodes of the thirteenth and fourteenth centuries are " capitalistic facts," which do not determine the character of an epoch. If a century in which one man, a St. Godric for example, behaves as a capitalist were to be called capitalistic, on what grounds should we deny that the nineteenth century, so often called, antonomastically, the " century of capitalism," was anti-capitalistic, since hidden away in the mountains there existed individuals who showed none of the qualities of the capitalist ?

On the other hand, we cannot dismiss as unimportant the question of precise period, when we would consider modern man in order to discover the spirit that informs him. It is certain that anyone who holds the capitalist

[1] J. Lemoine, " Les étrangers et le capitalisme en Belgique " in *Revue d'Histoire Economique et Sociale*, 1932, p. 266.

spirit to be the economic spirit that has informed men since the war, will not reach the same conclusions as to its origins and generative or determinant forces as those who by capitalist spirit understand the economic spirit informing Europeans in the middle of the nineteenth century. Unless, indulging in the superficial consideration that man always seeks the useful, he says, with Chlepner,[1] that the capitalist spirit is something immutable and constant. In which case the problem of its origin and ends would become identified with the problem of the origin and disappearance of man in the world, and only the Creator could enlighten us as to the causes of its emergence.

All this counsels us to be prudent and precise in our formulation of the problem, and to confine our research to a limited area. This does not mean that we cannot determine, as we shall determine, the nature of the economic spirit, known as the capitalist spirit, that has directed the actions of the majority of men, and, what is more, led to the re-organization of society, from the sixteenth century onwards.

2. Since the capitalist spirit is nothing but the prevailing economic spirit of a given period, it is as well for us to begin by defining the economic spirit.

By economic spirit we mean that complex inner attitude, conscious or subconscious, in virtue of which a man acts in a certain determined manner in business matters.

[1] B. S. Chlepner, *L'avenir du capitalisme*, p. 34.

Since every derivative human attitude is the result of some fundamental principle, the economic spirit of a given age is necessarily inseparable from the current idea of wealth and its ends. The current idea of wealth is reflected in the choice of means for obtaining it and of modes of using it. It follows that for every conception of wealth there are corresponding rules of economic conduct, which, when put into practice, determine the character of the economic actions performed by a given individual. In such actions the economic spirit of a man finds concrete expression, so much so that by observing them we can discover by what spirit he is moved. It is obvious that practical circumstances will tend to make the man of business either conform closely to what is the orthodox conception of wealth in his age or to draw away from it. And it is equally obvious that any degree of indulgence towards the solutions suggested by practical experience may in the long run permanently modify his attachment to such a conception.

It should be noted that the conception of wealth will be bound up with a general outlook on the universe, so that if this changes, the conception of wealth will also change. And since every age reveals the predominance of a given general outlook on the universe, it is easy to conclude that each age of history has its own particular idea of wealth and hence a special economic spirit.

Modern man, who is capitalistic, regards wealth as the best means for an ever more complete satisfaction of every conceivable need ; he also regards it as the best means for improving his own position. He considers goods as instruments to be used *ad libitum* by their possessor. He does not recognize any claim on them on the part of third parties not their possessors, still less does he think it unlawful for their possessor to use them so as to obtain an unlimited increase or their reproduction at ever diminishing cost.

Such a man will, indeed, associate an idea of duty with his idea of wealth, but this idea of duty, far from implying any limitation to his acquisition of wealth, will imply a mission to neglect nothing in order that his productive powers may yield the maximum results.[1] Once the bond is broken that united the idea of wealth as a means to the idea of eternal salvation as an end to be achieved subject to definite conditions regarding the use and acquisition of goods—once it has been asserted that there is no conflict between intensity of economic action and man's final end,[2] then the restrictions imposed by religious morality on the acquisition of wealth cease to exist.

---

[1] According to Weber (*Die prot. Ethik*, p. 36), the man informed by a capitalist spirit does not consider gain as a means for satisfying his material needs, but as the aim of life. Even granting this, we might still say that wealth is a means for satisfying the need for pure wealth felt by modern men.

[2] We may see one of the earliest public expressions of this conception in the protest of the eighteenth-century traders, who, affected by the prohibitions of loans at interest, declared that such loans were not only useful to society but moral in themselves. B. Groethuysen, *Origines de l'esprit bourgeois en France, I. L'Eglise et la bourgeoisie*, 2nd ed., Paris, Gallimard, 1927, p. 274. Also the anonymous author of *La Théorie de l'Intéret de l'argent* (p. 146), who explains : " La vraie raison, qui rend légitimes les profits que font les Banquiers, est donc qu'ils remplissent les devoirs d'un état ; que cet état est utile et autorisé. . . . Tout établissement d'une utilité reconnue par la société est aussi un établissement licite ; parce que la suprême Sagesse n'a pu mettre en opposition l'ordre des choses et les règles des mœurs."

Wealth no longer appears as a means to satisfy certain essential needs only in a limited degree. On the contrary, the conviction spreads that wealth is a means to be sought with whatever means may seem best, so long as it is desirable and possible to do so. This conception does not exclude the condemnation of certain means of gain, such as theft, blackmail, or robbery, but, unlike the pre-capitalist conception, it asserts that there is no limit to the use and perfecting of lawful means. This is a conclusion reached inasmuch as a quantitatively unlimited acquisition of wealth, or an unlimited satisfaction of needs, is no longer considered censurable.

Once the danger of an infringement of the moral law through over-intense use of lawful means is excluded, the economic law becomes the criterion of such use. Henceforth it is the principle of returns that regulates intensity in the use of morally lawful means. We can see how this is something of immense importance, for to admit a moral limitation to intensity in the use of morally lawful means is to bar the way to innumerable modes of enrichment, and, above all, it often means the prevention of the smallest increase in available quantity of wealth. To abandon this attitude implies the most decided condemnation of the traditionalism which Sombart[1] holds to be characteristic of the pre-capitalist spirit. And the new attitude is possible only when the principle of subsistence, or, better, of sufficiency, is repudiated.

[1] W. Sombart, *Der Bourgeois*, pp. 13–14.

The essence of the capitalist spirit becomes clearer if we reflect that the pre-capitalist who looked upon wealth as a social instrument, and who related a man's economic activity to the general requirements of his station in life, had to discriminate not only between lawful and unlawful means of acquiring wealth (a distinction that must be made, though with other criteria, by the capitalist also), but between lawful and unlawful intensity in the use of lawful means. For the pre-capitalist, morality not only condemns unlawful means, but limits the use of those that are lawful. Thus, it is plain, purely economic criteria cannot function; the rationalization of economic life is the result of moral criteria. And this because the pre-capitalist does not hold the unlimited enrichment of an individual to be lawful. Such enrichment would indeed seem to him senseless, since each has a strictly limited number of needs to be satisfied in the measure demanded by his station in life. And to better the latter would have seemed to the pre-capitalist unjustifiable.[1]

A man convinced that wealth is a means for the attainment of his individual, natural ends, which are not and cannot be divorced from his individual, supernatural ends or from the natural ends of society, will choose such means of acquiring wealth as will not lead him away from his ultimate end or from ends connected with it. In short, since the attainment of his individual end,

[1] For the authorities on which we base our description of the historical features of the pre-capitalist spirit, see our book, *Le origini dello spirito capitalistico in Italia.*

natural and supernatural, together with social ends, requires him to follow certain economic paths, chosen in the light of social and religious moral precepts, his economic activity must respect the rules of action that lead to the attainment of such ends. Economic activity, as an aspect of human action for the attainment of human ends, must take place within the moral sphere, which is circumscribed by social customs, political regulations, and religious principles. The means of acquiring goods will not therefore be classified as practicable or impracticable according to greater or smaller returns, but according to their conformity to the moral lines within which every action must be contained. It goes without saying that, when various means are equally lawful, that which will yield the best returns will be preferred. At bottom, then, the primary characteristic of the pre-capitalist spirit is that the choice of means of acquiring goods is determined by criteria, not of pure utility, but of utility only in so far as is compatible with the vigorous existence of extra-economic criteria. It seems almost superfluous to dwell at length on the primary characteristic of the capitalist spirit. Since the capitalist's moral code does not impose any limitation on the use of lawful and useful means, the primary characteristic of the capitalist spirit is the unlimited use of all means of acquiring wealth that are held to be morally lawful and economically useful. The capitalist does not rule out moral considerations. He adopts a moral code of his own, which, while it declares certain means to be unlawful (and in this is often in agreement with pre-capitalist mentality), does not limit the use of those means that are reputed lawful.[1]

Another difference between the mentality of the pre-capitalist and that of the capitalist is this : the former considers that appraisements of value in the economic sphere should be governed by moral criteria ; the latter would make the economic criterion the sole norm of such appraisements. Thus, for example, the pre-capitalist tends to make the price of an object correspond to the cost of its production, rather than to its value in general estimation [2], the capitalist measures the price of a commodity rather by general estimation than by the cost of production. Hence an article sold below cost represents a lawful exchange for the capitalist, while for the pre-capitalist the lawfulness of such exchange is at least open to grave doubt.

Another example. Whereas the pre-capitalist sought to equate wages rather to the needs of the worker than to his output, the capitalist, on the contrary, tends to base them rather on the worker's output than on his needs. This example shows how often the moral criterion intervenes in the economic appraisements of the

---

[1] It may not be useless to draw the reader's attention to the differences between what we have here written and what we wrote in Chap. VI of our work on the origins of the capitalist spirit. Nevertheless, the modification does not change our views on the time when the capitalistic spirit arose in Italy, nor on its causes.

[2] We find proofs of this in the rules of the mediæval guilds either on increase of prime cost or on the tally system. See Sapori's well-known study on the question, which we have already quoted. Also the examples we give in our *Origini dello spirito capitalistico*, Chaps. II and III.

pre-capitalist, and how, instead, those of the capitalist are governed by purely economic criteria.

The rules of religious and social morality accepted by the European pre-capitalist gave him an idea of wealth as a means for the attainment of the natural and supernatural ends both of him who had and him who had not. Thus this means was not so much given to the individual as to mankind. This idea is of the first importance, for it leads directly to a social conception of the use of wealth, that is, to a correlation of the satisfaction of a man's own needs with the satisfaction of those of his neighbour. This conception withheld him from unlimited personal enrichment. He might indeed acquire as much as he wished, but he could not enjoy as much as he wished. That which he had acquired, once he had satisfied his own needs—the persistence of which, given his religious and social status, would have impeded his orderly concentration on the attainment of his supreme end—he might not keep or use for himself, but was bound to dispense it to those in need; to give it back to be used by the society to which it belonged. There was thus a limit to the pre-capitalist's enjoyment of his goods, just as the current conception of wealth limited him in acquiring them, by ruling out means that were not reputed moral, and limiting the use of those that were moral. This twofold limitation sprang from the subordination of economic to extra-economic (politico-religious) ends.[1]

[1] For all that has been written, by ourselves and others, on pre-

A second characteristic, then, of the pre-capitalist spirit is the social use of wealth, which, for the individual, becomes a limitation to his enjoyment of wealth. This limitation might be spontaneous or enforced ; it implied conformity to social morality, which was guaranteed either by the laws of the Church or by civil laws.[1] It implied also a limitation in favour now of the super-natural ends of the individual, now of the natural ends of society, but always at the expense of natural-individual, or, more exactly, of purely economic ends.

The capitalist, on the contrary, has no social conception, but an individual and utilitarian conception of the use of wealth.[2] Thus unlimited possibilities of enjoyment make his capacity to acquire wealth equally unlimited. We can say, then, that another characteristic of the capitalist spirit is the individualistic and utilitarian use of wealth, and this becomes an unlimited enjoyment of wealth. Hence an added urge to the unlimited acquisition of wealth.

In summary, we may say that a fruit of the capitalist

capitalist mentality, see Chaps. I, II and VI of our *Origini dello spirito capitalistico.*

[1] Ecclesiastical legislation became the guarantor of pre-capitalist ideals when, for instance, it issued decrees against usurers, or demanded that at the usurer's death restitution of his usuries must be made. (A. Sapori, " L'interesse del denaro a Firenze nel Trecento " in *Archivio Storico Italiano,* 1928, vol. X.) Civil legislation did the same when it punished usury, supported the rules of the guilds, forbade competition, or guaranteed the just price in innumerable ways. (A. Fanfani, *Le origini,* pp. 52–65. Also a bibliography.)

[2] We speak of the perfect type of capitalist. In practice, a capitalist will have various qualities in varying degrees ; sometimes he will feel the influence of other ideas and sometimes he will not. He is a man living among men, and after men who did not all think and act as he.

spirit is that attitude adopted by a man towards the problems of wealth, its acquisition and use, when he holds that wealth is simply a means for the unlimited, individualistic and utilitarian satisfaction of all possible human needs. A man governed by this spirit will, in acquiring wealth, choose the most effectual means among such as are lawful, and will use them without any anxiety to keep the result within certain limits. In the use of wealth he will seek individualistic enjoyment; to the acquisition and enjoyment of goods he will recognize one limit only—hedonistic satiety.

Clearly, such a man will not believe that he has ever fully perfected the means of seeking and acquiring wealth. Hence another, derivative quality—the perfection of means, a perfecting that we may call "rationalization," though it is well to qualify it as "economic," for the concept of rational is relative.[1] The pre-capitalist is more traditionalist, that is, more attached to the means that he considers sufficient for his purpose. He is content with the good that he has, and will not seek for better, for the very simple reason that he is not troubled by a search for something that will bring in ever higher returns. As we have already observed, the idea of subsistence implies traditionalism; while that of unlimited production implies a dynamism, that is, an ever unsatisfied, ever increasing economic rationalization of means. We have pointed out elsewhere[2]

[1] M. Weber, *Die prot. Ethik*, p. 11.
[2] A. Fanfani, *Le origini*, p. 156.

that in a pre-capitalist system the moralist plays a considerable part, in appraising the means employed and either deciding in their favour or excluding them. In a capitalistic system the important roles belong to the engineer and economist, who judge means by their returns and on that basis adopt or reject them. All this explains why, though in the pre-capitalist period we find means fully adequate to the aims involved, and even an initial stage of economic rationality, within the limits allowed by the general rationality, the progressive perfecting of such means is a characteristic of the capitalist age in which it reaches a point that has allowed at least one author to point to rationality as the first of the distinctive characters of capitalism.[1]

It is in such differences of conception that we find the essential distinction between the capitalist and pre-capitalist spirit. And it is this differentiation that, above and beyond institutions, forms, economic means, allows us to declare whether a system is capitalistic or no.[2] In making this our testing-rod in distinguishing between one economic age and another, we do not leave out of account the differences of institutions, forms, technical means. On the contrary, we shall see how these are more or less closely and directly bound up with the prevailing economic conception. Nor does our approach

---

[1] M. M. Rossi, *L'ascesi capitalistica*, Rome, 1928, pp. 9–14.
[2] Weber (*Die prot. Ethik*, p. 34; Eng. tr., p. 19) points out that the capitalism that existed in China, India, and Babylonia, in classical times and in the Middle Ages, differs from our own by the particular ethos underlying it.

to the problem imply any denial that practical circumstances may determine a transition from one conception to another. If we did not pay attention to the diversity of underlying concepts that we have just discovered, and stopped short at the consideration of forms and technical means, we might say, with other writers, that capitalism existed on a considerable scale long before the period generally recognized as capitalistic. Granted, as we shall see in Chapter III, that where the capitalist spirit is strongly established, we find the development of certain, definite forms. But while the development of these forms is a consequence of its action, their first emergence is often simply the outcome of man's inventive genius and of his natural quest, in every phase of civilization, for the means best adapted to his purpose—a means which, for modern man, has never reached its final perfection. Certainly in a capitalist age much energy is expended on the improvement of means, and this improvement is governed by the economic end of highest and best returns.

Once for all, let us say that the capitalist spirit, like the pre-capitalist spirit, is not so much something concrete and continuous as a general trend of thought. Only by such an admission can we explain how one and the same man may now appear to be moved by a capitalist spirit, and a moment later, or better, in another deal or in other circumstances, no longer appear moved by that spirit.

Is it necessary to recall that in one and the same period we may find men moved by a capitalist spirit side by side with men moved by a pre-capitalist spirit ? We do not think so.[1] The fact is explained by the lack of uniformity in the social evolution of different strata of society, or of different regions, and also by the individual diversity of human personality.

All this might make it seem a hopeless task to identify a capitalistic or pre-capitalistic period, even in the restricted field of European society since the time of Christ. As a matter of fact, such identification is perfectly possible if we fix our attention on the predominance [2] of this or that ruling spirit, a predominance that has as result the permeation of the whole of society, with all its institutions, by the spirit directing the more numerous and more powerful of its members. For even those who are not touched by the prevailing spirit, or who are moved by another, must often—unless they hold themselves aloof from the economic world—live and act in accordance, not with their own convictions, but with the convictions of those who inspire and direct social institutions.[3] In any case, in a society in which two or more individuals have something to offer (supply), and x individuals require that something (demand), it is obvious that if one of the two in command of the commodity, in the absence of any impediment in

[1] Von Below, *Probleme der Wirtschaftsgeschichte*, p. 430.

[2] Sombart (*Der Bourgeois*, p. 16) writes that we must look for a predominance, since no period is exclusively governed by a single spirit.

[3] " The present capitalist system is an immense cosmos, into which the individual is born and which is presented to him, at least in so far as he is an individual, as an immutable environment in which he must live " (M. Weber, *Die prot. Ethik*)

the civil law (the only law that has coercive force to-day), puts himself in a position to supply those who require it with greater ease, his competitors will be obliged to imitate him under pain of serious losses, even if to do so they will have to do violence to convictions or ideals to which they would normally have remained faithful.[1] This series of observations explains the fact that in a pre-capitalist period we find men who are moved by a capitalistic spirit. The opposite has come about in the more recent period that is known as that of modern capitalism.[2] This co-existence of different spirits need not prevent us from characterizing a period as capitalist or pre-capitalist, for in each period the ruling class and the social institutions, working in or in accordance with a certain spirit, will hinder or censure or prevent the working of another. In a pre-capitalist age a man seeking individualistic enjoyment of wealth is accused of being a miser ; a man who acquires wealth by means that are held to be unlawful, or even by the unlimited use of lawful means, is condemned.[3] In a capitalist age a man

---

[1] I remember that in a little village in Tuscany there were only two bakeries. The owner of the one wished to close on Sunday, but was unable to do so because his rival kept open, and had he himself failed to follow suit he would have lost his customers who, being restaurant-keepers, wanted fresh bread on Sundays as well as week-days.

[2] When in 1776 there was question of establishing a discounting bank in France (see Bachaumont, *Mémoires secrètes*, vol. 9, p. 111), various doctors of the Sorbonne sought to oppose the scheme, appealing to pre-capitalist conceptions. Some ten years before we learn from a decree of 1761 that the first timid appearance of advertisement on behalf of trade was not looked upon with any favour (R. Bigo, *La Caisse d'Escompte*, 1776-93, Paris, Les Presses Univ. de France, pp. 49 and 96-97).

[3] Cf. A. Fanfani, *Le origini*, etc., Chaps. I and II, which give concrete instances.

seeking to acquire wealth solely by means that, as estimated by pre-capitalist mentality, appear lawful, will probably very soon have to retire from business.

It is not to be inferred from this that the means used by capitalists are immoral. We merely say that the capitalist's unlimited use of even lawful means would not be approved of by the pre-capitalist.

3. Before pursuing our analysis, it is necessary to put forward certain other observations that should forestall possible objections. Some might think that we believed in an instantaneous substitution of a capitalistic for a pre-capitalistic spirit. Others might think that we claim to have discovered a cause that determined overnight such an instantaneous substitution of economic spirit. Such suppositions, as the reader will see, are very far from our thought. Indeed, we hold that only by degrees did the capitalist spirit attain its unparalleled dominance in the last years of the nineteenth century, and we consider that this development was able to come about in successive periods through various combinations of circumstances, now of the material order, now of the spiritual.

Undoubtedly it was in a pre-capitalistic period that some Tom or Dick first felt himself drawn to a capitalistic mode of thought, and hence to capitalistic action. Pirenne's correct observation that St. Godric in the seventh century was moved by a capitalistic spirit, and Heynen's equally correct reference to the members of the Mairano family in the eleventh century, thus acquire the following significance : here were definite individual examples of men in whom the capitalistic mode of thought and action first declared itself, without finding its way barred by other principles. Then come the twelfth and thirteenth centuries. The number of individuals who yield to the lure of capitalism increases, though there are few who fail to repent either on their death-beds or during life, and by such repentance reaffirm their fundamental attachment to a belief in the spiritual principles of pre-capitalism. But as the number of individuals who act in a capitalistic manner gradually increases, such repentance grows ever more rare. Capitalistic acts follow one another with increasing frequency, till they form a long series, no longer interrupted by moments in which the individual returns to the law or to his old belief, repudiating the new ones in a single act. Christians begin to die without anxiety as to the next world. A dying usurer will even urge his sons, who exhort him to make restitution of the fruits of his usury, to look after the devils in this world, for he himself will look after those in the next.[1] By the end of the fifteenth century no one feels shame if he acts in a capitalistic manner. The younger men, swept along by the new current, drag the old ones with them. Capitalists seek to break down the barriers that civil

---

[1] A usurer once replied to his children, who were urging him to think of his soul : " You take care of the devils in this world, and leave me to deal with those in the next " (Tamassia, *La famiglia italiana nel sec. XV e XVI*, Palermo, 1928, pp. 28–30).

and ecclesiastical legislation set to their action. From now on there is no need to follow, even in synthesis, the struggle between the capitalist spirit, which reigns uncontested in the minds of men, and social institutions, imbued with a pre-capitalistic spirit which though formally modified is substantially unchanged. At bottom the mercantile period is merely the period in which, under the guise of political aims, a non-capitalistic spirit informs social institutions,[1] and leads them to protect and foster economic agencies already informed by a capitalistic spirit. For quite a time these do not appear to conflict with the non-capitalistic institutions, for the simple reason that the latter, starting from other principles, seeking other aims, guarantee the persistence of conditions highly favourable to their development. When towards the end of the eighteenth century an outcry is raised against the mercantile system [2]—not through any aggravation of its burdens, but through the growing vigour of the aspirations of those on whom they fell—the struggle between the politico-social pre-capitalism of the State and the capitalism of individuals

[1] According to Lipson (*The Economic History of England*, 5th ed., London, 1929, vol. I, p. 491), protection and monopoly were granted by the state to the Merchant Adventurers in order to ensure the development of " a well-ordered and ruled trade " according to " the ideal of mediæval commerce." The mercantile system in France pursued similar aims (P. Boissonnade, *Le socialisme d'Etat, L'industrie et les classes industrielles en France pendant les deux premiers siècles de l'ère moderne* (1493–1661), Paris, 1927, pp. 9–10).

Sombart (*Der moderne Kapitalismus*, I, pp. 362–393) connects mercantilism with the economic policy of the mediæval cities from which Luzzatto (*Storia economica*, 1934, p. 428) and Heckscher (*Der Merkantilismus*, Jena, 1932) hold that it derived its guiding principles.

[2] G. De Ruggiero, *Storia del liberalismo moderno*, Bari, 1925.

would be openly renewed; the capitalist spirit would make its last and most successful attempt to gain possession of the whole of society. After this victory, individuals, doctrines, the State would all be imbued with it, and the capitalist spirit would have its hour of triumph. The capitalist system would receive the final retouches necessary to perfect it and bring it to its apogee.[1] Thus the development of the capitalist spirit occupies nearly ten centuries, from the ninth to the eighteenth, in the course of which it passes from the stage of timid and sporadic appearances in isolated individuals to that in which it is firmly established in nearly the whole of the ruling classes, in doctrines, in society, and in all social institutions.

We shall now see, albeit briefly, what combinations of circumstances in the course of these ten centuries from time to time either facilitated or hindered the trend towards the capitalist mode of thought and life; hence towards the capitalist economic, or, better, social system.

In a period in which a given economic spirit prevails—let us take, for instance, that of the pre-capitalist spirit—we find circumstances that induce the individual to forsake the traditional spirit, directing him in a particular sense, which consciously or unconsciously is determined by a new mode of thought, a new way of envisaging life, so new that it conflicts with the old, so new that it leads to actions condemned by those who are

---

[1] " The triumph of capitalist organization is not earlier than the XIX century, and for the most part not earlier than the middle of that century " (Sée, *Les origines du capitalisme*, p. 7).

37

still swayed by the old economic spirit that was the soul of pre-capitalistic society. It is obvious that such circumstances, occurring in a pre-capitalist period, conduce to action in opposition to the spirit of the time. Some of these circumstances lead, and in fact led, to action in a capitalistic sense, stimulating what we may call the capitalist spirit. Thus, for example, increased possibility of losses, growing risks, drive men to a desperate defence of their goods, their interests. The risk may become such as to lead them, in their eagerness to defend their interests, to overstep those limits of which pre-capitalistic canons and convictions advised or prescribed respect. We could here bring forward many cogent examples, and all would prove the truth of the assertion at the base of the present argument.

In a pre-capitalistic age we find also many circumstances of a spiritual order that directly draw man away from the pre-capitalist spirit and indirectly lead him to approach the capitalistic mode of thought. Thus in mediæval pre-capitalist society, in which the rationality of economic action did not depend solely on economic criteria, but on economic criteria circumscribed by social and religious, that is to say, by extra-economic criteria, a decline in faith in religious beliefs brought about a lessened attachment to the economic spirit, hence to the economic reasoning that found in such belief a powerful buttress and perhaps its *raison d'être*.

Circumstances material and spiritual, to be noted on various occasions, sometimes in combination, sometimes

38

working separately, with predominance of effects now of the one, now of the other, are facts that explain how a group of men came to break away from the pre-capitalist mode of thought, to adapt themselves to the mode of thought we call capitalist.

To some it may seem as if what we have defined as the spirit of capitalism were an imaginary category, since no agent in the capitalistic world of to-day would now dream of justifying his mode of action by similar arguments. But this objection we may meet by referring to Weber's conclusive statement: " to-day it is no longer necessary to seek the support of an ethical force, but instead the *Weltanschauung* is determined by the positions of politico-commercial and politico-social interests ; the man who, in the actions of life, does not adapt himself to the conditions indispensable to success under the capitalistic system, is left behind or goes under." [1]

It has seemed to us supremely important to sum up these considerations, to dispel the impression that the capitalistic spirit appeared to us as something miraculous, suddenly sprung up out of nothing, that overnight gained mastery of the minds of men, who, for no reason at all, allowed it to invade their minds, as a jug is filled with water. We were particularly anxious to emphasize that the economic spirit is not a phenomenon that finds man a passive victim, as in the eruption of a volcano or the disappearance of an island in the sea, but a

[1] M. Weber, *Die prot. Ethik.*

phenomenon which in part man voluntarily brings about and in part does not resist, and which comes about in man himself. It is essentially a human phenomenon, which outwardly reveals itself only in its expressions and effects. It is a spiritual phenomenon which came about in man, and then transformed the life of men and the structure of society.

CHAPTER III

INSTRUMENTS OF CAPITALISM

1. Spread of capitalist spirit. 2. Pre-capitalist institutions as foundations for progress of capitalist spirit. 3. The minimum means in the labour sphere. 4. Rationalization of the workshop. 5. Finance. 6. Capture of the market.

1. AT the end of the last chapter we thought well to point out that the capitalist spirit at first showed itself transiently in a few individuals, then inspired their actions more frequently, and ended by informing their whole lives. Such individuals exerted an influence on their contemporaries, drawing in their wake a large number, and these, increasing with the passage of time and the succession of generations, at a given moment were able to wield a preponderant influence in public organizations, to adapt social institutions to the new spirit, to take possession of the State and subordinate it to the new ideals,[1] in short, to make society capitalist.

In this connection, the figure of Jacques Cœur (1393–1456) is typical. A merchant, he builds the ships he uses. He sets up warehouses in various trading centres. He manufactures the goods in which he trades. He establishes relations with the court of Charles VII

[1] For the influence of the industrial bourgeoisie on French economic policy in the fifteenth century, see P. Boissonnade, *Le socialisme d'Etat*, p. 18.

41

of France, becoming its treasurer and obtaining from the King special facilities for engaging his crews and ordinances which, by abolishing tolls and promoting an improvement of roads and water-ways, help the development of his immense trade. Thus, by indirect methods, Jacques Cœur made the might and power of the sovereign serve his own purpose and that of those who, as his subordinates or following in his footsteps, revived the economic life of France. This French neo-capitalist was able to turn even the authority of the Church to his advantage; from Nicholas V he obtained a wide licence to trade with infidels.[1]

The process, which we have briefly summarized, and of which the capitalistic action of Jacques Cœur provides a partial illustration, occupied many centuries. Before they could make society capitalistic, the several individuals who sought capitalistic ends would strive to provide themselves with means and instruments capable of compassing such ends. To begin with, there is an attempt to adapt old means to serve capitalistic ends, as we see in the increasing perfection of company contracts.[2] This attempt at the individual modification of old instruments will continue, almost unobserved; only when social institutions prevent the modification of such instruments in a capitalistic sense will capitalistic

---

[1] See R. Bouvier, *Jacques Cœur*, Paris, 1928. Especially pp. 58–61, 70–7, 89.

[2] L. Goldschmidt, *Universalgeschichte des Handelsrechts*, 1891. F. Schupfer, *Il diritto delle obbligazioni in Italia nell'età del Risorgimento*, Turin, III, pp. 158–61, 1921.

individuals feel the necessity of shaping the social institutions to their own ends. For instance, only when it becomes desirable to lend money at interest does the prohibition of such transactions become a burden. Then, when a thousand expedients to escape the penalties involved, or to make amends for evil committed have been tried, when even the arguments of the Schools, which left a wide loophole for various claims for compensation for money lent, no longer satisfy, comes the demand that the political or religious authorities shall explicitly repeal their previous prohibitions.[1] Or, again, when it is considered desirable to propitiate a customer by special concessions, or to adopt a system of deferred payment, which guild regulations forbade, at first attempts are made to induce the guilds to relax their ruling, and finally, in order to obtain full freedom in this and other fields, the demand is made for the dissolution of the guilds themselves.

The attempt to organize society on a capitalistic basis begins when attacks are made on pre-capitalist social institutions, and this attempt is only an episode in the action of men, moved by a capitalistic spirit, to procure the instruments and *milieu* that will enable them to attain the ends they seek. This is almost too obvious to need statement, once we realize that for every man, and

---

[1] We have elsewhere given our authorities for these assertions as to the attempts to conceal usury, attempts at reparation, the theories on usury, State permits to usurers, and the fixing of legal rates of interest. (See *Le origini dello spirito capitalistico*, p. 35, and *Scisma e spirito capitalistico in Inghilterra*, passim.)

hence also for the man informed by a capitalistic spirit, society is merely a complexus of instruments and means, organized for the attainment of given ends.

The capitalistic man, who is no longer bound to the idea of sufficiency, devotes himself before all else to perfecting the tools used. At first he modifies the old ones. Then, dissatisfied with the limited returns achieved by the improved tools, he turns to seek for novelties. Into the usages of trade and industry he seeks to introduce the new capitalistic logic. He becomes the propagandist of his mode of thought, forces his competitors to imitate his new mode of behaviour, imposes or ensures the acceptance of the new usages, the new formalities, and, since these are favourable and advantageous to those only who possess adequate plant, any man who accepts the relations imposed and spread by the new capitalist must speedily put himself in a position to accept the new plant also. The introduction of advertisement, for example, becomes an advantage only to those who wish and are able to make continual improvements in the process of production. The abolition of price conventions marks the economic death of the producer who cannot cut his costs. The discontinuance of prescribed methods of manufacture leaves the shrewd producer free to seek for novelties, and forces the tardy or backward producer to do the same. When there is no longer an obligation to respect feast-days, the man attached to the feast-day rest is faced with the dilemma of whether he will respect the feast and suffer economic loss in consequence, or whether he will omit to do so and continue to make money in competition with the man who cares little for feast-day rest.

Since the new economic usages cannot be introduced into a life attuned to the old spirit, life in general and social custom must perforce be modified, so that at no period shall social life take a course incompatible with the new criterion that informs the activity of capitalistically minded individuals.

Capitalistic social life, capitalistic individual life, cannot develop if a cultural life in opposition to them persists. Hence the fact that, as the capitalistic mode of life spreads, theories are pressed into its service now to justify it, now to exalt it, now to propagate it, and now to perfect it. The series of the theorists of capitalistic virtues begins with Jean Quidort,[1] continues with Leon Battista Alberti,[2] with Calvin, in regard to certain aspects,[3] with all the champions of the mercantile system, in regard to others—though their fundamental thesis of the subordination of economics to politics is, to say the least, non-capitalistic.[4] Then come Bernard

---

[1] A. Dempf, *Sacrum imperium*, Munich and Berlin, 1929, pp. 422–5. Dempf finds in the Parisian Jean Quidort (d. 1306) the theory of the *homo economicus* as the basis of the State (J. Quidort, *De potestate regia et papali*).

[2] Weber (*Die prot. Ethik*, Chap. I, sec. 2, Eng. tr., p. 56) was the first to consider Alberti's work from this point of view. Sombart (*Der Bourgeois*, pp. 161–2, Eng. tr., pp. 223–7) extends the analysis and makes Alberti the mediæval champion of the capitalist spirit. We have recently re-examined the question in Chap. V of *Le origini*.

[3] H. Hauser, *Les débuts du capitalisme*, Chap. II.

[4] Fanfani, "I presupposti delle dottrine economiche presmithiane" in *Economia*, May, 1933.

45

Mandeville,[1] Benjamin Franklin,[2] Condorcet[3]; then all the physiocrats and the theorists of *laissez faire*, whose doctrines most assuredly do not clash with capitalistic ideals.[4]

Once the mastery of culture has been achieved, there remains the State. It is to the mastery of the State that the agents and theorists of capitalism now apply themselves. The State is the last social instrument to be modified, and this modification is essential if all the other instruments are to function not in an atmosphere of conflict, but in one that is fully propitious to their working. Only so can maximum results be obtained. The evils of the world—so say eighteenth-century eulogists of the capitalist mentality—are not to be attributed to men and their instincts, but to the State, which, in opposition to human actions and human ends, aims at other goals altogether. The State, the last complex instrument to be mastered by capitalism, must not itself act. Let it prepare the ground by guaranteeing *security;* let it predispose the minds of men by *education*; and let it establish *freedom*, so that the economic machine, as transformed and to be transformed still further by the individual,[5] may so function as to achieve the maximum

---

[1] B. Mandeville, *The Fable of the Bees*, London, Parker, 1723. On Mandeville, see the essay by A. Schatz : " Bernard de Mandeville " in *Vierteljahrschrift für Sozial- und Wirtschaftsgeschichte*, 1903, vol. I, pp. 440 sq.

[2] Sombart, *Der Bourgeois*, Chap. II, Eng. tr. Chap. VII, pp. 103–24.

[3] Condorcet shows a capitalist and bourgeois mentality in his *Esquisse d'un tableau historique des progrès de l'esprit humain*.

[4] P. Mantoux, *La révolution industrielle au XVIII siècle*, Paris, Bellais, 1905, p. 486, Eng. tr. *The Industrial Revolution in the Eighteenth Century*, London, 1928, pp. 475–6. Also G. O'Brien, *An Essay*, op. cit., pp. 81–90.

[5] For the theories of the physiocrats, in so far as they are relevant to our

of economic rationalization that will mark the triumph of the capitalist spirit.

Thus, starting in the workshop of the first capitalistic manufacturer, the new economic spirit spreads a sense of the need for new instruments first in the group formed by his trade-associates, then in that of his fellow-citizens, then in that of his compatriots, till the whole mercantile class feels an impellent need to give a capitalistic orientation to the supreme machine of every society, the State.[1] When all had been transformed in a capitalist sense, it was needful to harmonize its workings, and this harmony could only be brought about by mastery of the State. All the works of the new social clock were ready, but the clock-case that was to contain them was ill-made, prevented synchronous movement, so that the capitalistic machinery worked in fits and starts, now swiftly, now slowly, and now might stand still. The clock-maker, namely, the capitalist, set to work, and made the new and appropriate clock-case the day on which the old clock-maker, the pre-capitalist, withdrew that which was appropriate no longer. The teeth of the separate wheels had been changed one by one; then new wheels had been fitted, then new pivots, new main springs, new balance-wheels, and, finally, a new clock-case, which,

problem, see G. Weulersse, *Le mouvement physiocratique en France de 1756 à 1770*, Paris, Alcan, 1910, vol. II, Chap. I.

[1] For propaganda in favour of capitalist and bourgeois theories of liberty and individualism at the end of the seventeenth and beginning of the nineteenth centuries, see A. Gerbi, *La politica del Settecento*, Bari, 1927, pp. 25–6, and D. Mornet, *Les origines intellectuelles de la Révolution Française (1715–87)*, Paris, 1933, passim.

47

containing all, enabled all to give the result desired.
Thus the capitalist spirit formed capitalistic means. As
a matter of fact, between spirit and means the relationship is not one of pure succession; the creation of
capitalistic means did not wait for the complete establishment of the capitalist spirit. The new spirit dawns,
declares itself, and modifies the means. The means,
thus modified, exert a pressure on the wills of men,
making them more ready to accept the requirements of
the new order, of which the capitalist spirit is both
motive force and expression. Thus, for example, when
the capitalist spirit, as it asserts itself more and more,
drives the producer to replace manual labour by
machinery, it creates new conditions; it creates new
instruments which, from the economic point of view,
rationalize production, increase it in obedience to
purely economic criteria, and hence enable capitalistic
ends to be achieved. But at the same time these new
instruments, inasmuch as they represent frozen capital,
require a certain margin of profit to set against expense
of working, and material and technical depreciation.
Such requirements, the less easy to satisfy in view of
competition, which increases risks, exert a moral pressure
on the will of the contractor, and drive him to further
rationalization, to continuous improvements. Thus the
fruit of capitalistic action leads to fresh progress towards
the full maturity of the capitalist spirit. Spirit and means
react one on the other. It is only for the sake of convenience that we are considering one at a time, noting

how both have corresponded to capitalistic ends, and how they have been gradually elaborated, with continuous improvements, so as to correspond ever better to such ends.

2. In the age previous to the advent of the capitalist spirit—understood as a social force and not as an individual urge to action—all means of private economic activity and all social institutions are either chosen or limited in working in view of pre-capitalist ends. In general, the aspirations of mediæval Europeans do not lead them to seek a purely economic rationality in the development of economic life. On the contrary, even in economic life, especially in its public aspect, the guiding criteria are not always economic. More often they are extra-economic—moral, political, religious— and intervene to limit the influence of economic standards on the selection of means and on the purposes and intensity of their use. In final analysis, these extra-economic criteria were the key-note of the economic order that came into being, whether private or collective.

The pre-capitalist age is the period in which definite social institutions, such as, for instance, the Church, the State, the Guild, act as guardians of an economic order that is not based on criteria of individual economic utility.[1] The Corporation or Guild is typical of the

[1] Doren (*Studien aus der Florentiner Wirtschaftsgeschichte*, vol. II, Stuttgart, 1908, p. 600) illustrates the various means of controlling the workmanship of the Florentine artisans.

period. It is the guardian of a system of economic activity in which the purely economic interests of the individual are sacrificed either to the moral and religious interests of the individual—the attainment of which is under the control of special public institutions—or to the economic and extra-economic interests of the community. Competition was restricted[1]; the distribution of customers, hence a minimum of work, was assured[2]; a certain system of work was compulsory[3]; trade with various groups might be forbidden for political or religious reasons[4]; certain practices

[1] Typical proofs of this limitation are to be found in some of the clauses (I, 14–6) of the Statutes of the Guild of Innkeepers of Florence (*Archivio di Stato*, Florence, *Statuti dell'Arte degli Albergatori*, I, 1324; IV, 1357).

[2] R. Broglio d'Aiano, " Sulle corporazioni medioevali delle arti in Italia e loro statuti " in *Rivista Internazionale di Scienze Sociali*, 1911, vol. 57, pp. 161–3; P. Gaudenzi, *Statuti delle Società del popolo di Bologna*, Bologna, 1896, p. 231; Fanfani, " Le arti di Sansepolcro " in *Rivista Internazionale di Scienze Sociali*, 1933, p. 156. For further details, see Fanfani, *Le origini*, etc., pp. 29–57.

[3] The Florentine druggists were forbidden to adulterate their goods (R. Ciasca, *L'arte dei medici e speziali nella storia e nel commercio fiorentino*, Florence, 1927, pp. 247–8). The Venetian tailors had to return pieces of cloth left over (P. Molmenti, *Storia di Venezia*, Bergamo, 1926, vol. I, p. 151). The bakers of Caprese were obliged to follow certain regulations in making bread (G. Chinali, *Caprese*, Arezzo, 1904); the same is true of the bakers of Carrara (*Stat. di Carrara*, lib. I, par. 3, in A. Angeli, *Carrara nel medioevo*, 1929, vol. 54, Fas. II). The leather-workers of Pistoia were forbidden to use leather which had been lying too long in the tannery (L. Zdekauer, *Statutum potestatis communis Pistorii, anni MCCLXXXXVI*, Milan, 1888, lib. III, Cap. LX).

[4] Frederick II forbade the Genoese to provide transport for members of the Council called by Gregory IX (F. Poggi, " Sopra alcune recenti pubblicazioni estere riguardanti il commercio di Genova " in *Atti della Società ligure di storia patria*, Genoa, 1924, vol. 52, p. 354). Peter of Aragon forbade Florentines to trade in his kingdom (A. Segre, *Storia del Commercio*, Turin, 1923, vol. I, p. 183). There is no need for us to give further examples. Everyone will recall how the Popes forbade Christians to trade in certain commodities during special periods, or with the Turks, or with the subjects of sovereigns in conflict with Rome. And all will recall how States used to forbid trade as a result of or a preliminary to military hostilities.

were compulsory, and working hours were limited[1];
there were a number of compulsory feasts[2]; prices
and rates of increase were fixed[3]; measures were taken
to prevent speculation.[4] Food laws and sumptuary
laws prove the impossibility and unlawfulness of an
economic activity governed by standards of purely
individual utility. Ecclesiastical and civil legislation
forestalled such a possibility, and dealt with the just
price[5] and usury. Plainly, all these institutions, and
many others that we could quote if the scope of the
present work permitted, reveal the influence of extra-
economic ideas and mark their paramount influence as
principles of rationality, in the economic life both of the
individual and of the community. And it is these institutions that guarantee that the means employed in economic
life shall conform to such principles, even if individuals
are unwilling to remain faithful to this order.[6] But

[1] Night work was forbidden, and thus there were fixed working hours,
varying with the season. For an instance, see P. Sella, op. cit., vol. I, pp. 242
sq. Other examples may be found in all mediæval statute books.
[2] For the many sources relating to this question, and for our criticism of
Sombart's arbitrary interpretations (in *Der Bourgeois*, pp. 19–20, and *Der
moderne Kapitalismus*, vol. I, part I, p. 37), see A. Fanfani, *Le origini*, pp. 62–6.
[3] A. Sapori, *Il " taccamento " di panni franceschi a Firenze nel Trecento* in
the volume " In onore di G. Prato," Turin, 1931, *Una compagnia di Calimala ai
primi del Trecento*, Florence, Olschki, 1932. For Florence, see also A. Doren,
Studien, vol. II, p. 564. For Venice, see P. Molmenti, op. cit., vol. I, p. 152.
[4] G. Arias, *I trattati commerciali della repubblica fiorentina*, Florence, 1901,
I, pp. 271 sq. P. Bonfante, *Lezioni di storia del commercio*, Rome, 1926, I,
p. 240. R. Caggese, *Un comune libero alle porte di Firenze nel secolo XIII*,
Florence, 1905, p. 170. A. Schaube, *Handelsgeschichte der romanischen
Völker des Mittelmeergebiets bis zum Ende der Kreuzzüge*, 1903, p. 773.
[5] A. Sapori, " Il giusto prezzo nella dottrina di San Tommaso e nella
pratica del suo tempo " in *Archivio Storico Italiano*, 1932.
[6] For economic organization in the pre-capitalist age in Belgium, see L.
Dechesne, *Histoire économique et sociale de la Belgique*, Liége, 1932, pp. 132–44.
For Italy see our own study, *Le origini*, etc.

more often than not the true guarantee of the use of such means was provided by the triumph of the pre-capitalist spirit in the minds of the many.

The capitalist spirit, by substituting other ends, made men dissatisfied with the old means and old institutions that had been adequate in the pre-capitalist system. All this became possible, because, with the advent, or, as we shall see more clearly in the following chapters, with the stable justification of the capitalist spirit, a new conception of the rationality of economic life enters the world. The economic order is established, not in obedience to extra-economic and extra-individual criteria, but in obedience to economico-individual criteria.

The triumph of this new rationality could only be brought about by adapting the old pre-capitalist instruments to the new capitalistic ends. They too had to be rationalized in accordance with the new conception. And this would have been impossible without the abolition of those institutions that defended and guaranteed the old rationality.

At bottom, the triumph of the new rationality depended on the abolition of those institutions that still defended the influence of political, social, and moral ideas on individual economic activity, limiting its autonomy and reducing its material results.

The rationalization of means employed by individuals and the purge of social institutions, which began in the fourteenth and fifteenth centuries—as we see from the new trend in the economic policy of the States and the

Guilds—in Europe took about three centuries, from 1500 to 1800, during which time "capitalism . . . is one of the prime forces moving and transforming the world."[1] The two processes neither follow one another nor alternate, but are interwoven. For our own convenience, we speak first of one, then of the other. If it would not imply a sacrifice of clarity, and if we did not prefer the method we have chosen, we could treat the two together. Our work would then be rather a chronological narrative of events than a logical investigation of the developments and forces that carried capitalism to its zenith.

Todd has recently protested against those who believe that "the industrial revolution is a kind of Grand Cañon, with an entry in the eighteenth century and an exit in the twentieth." We may adopt his protest, and extend it to include those who think they can tell us the year, if not the day, in which capitalism began, and even the hour in which it came or will come to an end !

In the case of either the industrial revolution or the growth of capitalism, we are faced by historical phenomena of which the evolution is slow and prolonged, and of which the manifestations, as Todd has noted in regard to the first, are as a rule only perceived when they have already existed for centuries.[2]

3. Rationalization determined by an individualistic

---

[1] K. Kaser, *L'età dell'assolutismo*, p. 32.
[2] A. J. Todd, *Industry and Society*, New York, 1933, p. 53.

economic criterion, which becomes the criterion of the best returns, in an early period shows itself in regard to the tools employed by single individuals. The reason for this is plain when we remember that the economic spirit, as we said in Chapter II, first reveals itself in a few individuals, and only as the number of those who accept it grows, does it become a collective spiritual phenomenon.

The economico-individualistic rationalization of means, that is, the choice of the means that is economically most profitable and its exploitation up to the limit that is economically desirable, comes about through inventions and improvements both in tools and plant, and in the organization of business. But action in this sense is not to be found till a later period of history, and in many spheres not till our own time. In the earliest branches of production in which we find it, it did not take place on any scale worth noting till after the first half of the eighteenth century. Before that, especially in the fifteenth and sixteenth and even in the seventeenth centuries, the rationalizing of means for capitalistic ends is neither clearly discernible nor continuous.[1] Thus, for example, the technical division of labour came only very late. For a long time, as Hauser has pointed out, division according to trade persists.[2] Improvements

[1] For the development and motives ("thirst for gain, spirit of adventure, desire for novelty") of the early inventions of the fifteenth and sixteenth centuries, see G. Luzzatto, *Storia economica*, pp. 39–40. For inventions and technical appliances of the sixteenth and seventeenth centuries, see W. Sombart, "Die Technik im Zeitalter des Frühkapitalismus" in *Archiv für Sozialwissenschaft und Sozialpolitik*, vol. XXXIV, 1912.

[2] Hauser, *Les débuts*, p. 13. Technical division of labour was, however, already in practice in 1455 among the miners of Lyons.

in tools are slow and rare. Up till the seventeenth
century money was still struck with a hammer die !
And though as early as the fifteenth century the water-
mill was used as motive power in paper-mills and forges,[1]
more often instead of seeking for the best result by the
use of more appropriate instruments, manufacturers
sought it by the use of spurious means, and, indeed, in
the greater number of cases, by an attempt to obtain
privileged positions in which they could achieve magnificent results without any innovations in the processes
of production.[2]

But all these expedients, which certainly were
employed, should not lead us to think that in the early
centuries of the modern period the capitalist spirit
operated only in this primitive manner. The reality is
rather different, for, side by side with such actions as we
have quoted, the very beginning of modern times saw
also the first attempts at a real and proper rationalization of means in order to achieve—apart from privileged
positions more or less lawfully obtained—that maximum
individual economic profit that is the goal of the capitalist
spirit. We can none the less assert that when the quest
for improvements becomes more intense, this increase
in potentiality is connected with the new economic
spirit. Indeed, it is the capitalist spirit that, by eliminat-

---

[1] Lipson (*The Economic History of England*, vol. I, p. 426) gives examples
of hostility towards the introduction of machinery into England in the
fourteenth and fifteenth centuries.

[2] On the importance of the patents and privileges granted to manufacturers from the fifteenth century onwards, see Hauser, " Le travail dans
l'ancienne France," part III, in *Les débuts*, op. cit.

ing all extra-economic restrictions, favours improvements in tools and appliances, and encourages them by establishing an economic maximum as goal.

Once a man has become imbued with the capitalist spirit, his chief concern in regard to work is indeed to obtain the maximum results with the minimum means, but since, in appraising that maximum and minimum, he has to consider only economico-individual standards, he will have greater freedom of action and a wider choice—a choice unhampered in any way by extra-economic obligations. Such a man, possessed by a crude capitalistic spirit, and without any sound and mature criterion of discernment, instead of seeking for the best returns in the sphere of production, that is to say, by reducing costs to a minimum through the use of improved plant, will seek it—as many actually sought it —in a reduction of the cost of raw materials, so that he secretly substitutes material of inferior quality for material of good quality, to the immediate detriment of the unwitting consumer, but with ultimate detriment to himself. The weavers of gold tissue of Lyons, in order to compete with those of Paris, instead of weaving their imitation gold on thread wove it on silk as though it were true gold, contrary to the rules of the craft which the Parisian workers respected.[1] In Flanders in the sixteenth century the rural workshops launched inferior

---

[1] Hauser, "Les questions industrielles et commerciales dans les cahiers de la Ville et des communautés de Paris aux Etats généraux de 1614" in *Vierteljahrschrift für Sozial- und Wirtschaftsgeschichte*, I, 1, 903, pp. 376–80 and 392–6.

products on the market, as cheap counterfeits of those manufactured by their urban rivals.[1] In 1578 at Antwerp the cloth-dyers, contrary to regulations, used Barbary aniline and Portingade indigo, which spoiled the work by burning the fabric.[2] In England as early as 1390 there are complaints, which Lipson considers well founded, against similar more or less dishonest means of gain.[3] But there were also others. In the same category we may place attempts to obtain minimum costs by reducing the quality of the workmanship. It is clear that it was not possible to continue long on such a road, but it was on precisely this road that the first capitalists made certain attempts to introduce means adequate to their ends. Assuredly, such means were the least costly in appearance only; time and experience made them appear as makeshifts inadequate to the attainment of the capitalistic goal, and they were abandoned.

At a period that is more or less near our own, according to which of the various European countries we consider, attempts were made to obtain minimum costs and maximum output not by the more intensive utilization of technical means, but by a maximum exploitation of the worker. This maximum exploitation was achieved in two ways: either by a maximum of hours of

---

[1] Pirenne, "Note sur la fabrication des tapisseries en Flandres au XVI siècle" in *Viert. für So₹. u. W.*, 1906, p. 336.

[2] G. Faignez, *L'économie sociale de la France sous Henri IV* (1589–1610), Paris, 1897, p. 378.

[3] Lipson, *Economic History of England*, vol. I, p. 425.

57

work,[1] or by reducing wages to a rock-bottom minimum.[2] The real value of wages was often diminished by the adoption of the truck system,[3] or the employer could recoup himself by defrauding the workers in the measurement of the material entrusted to them to work.[4]

The better to achieve both a maximum of hours and a minimum of wages, not seldom—indeed, in some countries it was the general rule, especially when the introduction of machinery and the division of labour made it more feasible—female[5] and child

[1] In North Wales in the eighteenth century miners worked more than twelve hours a day (H. Dodd, *The Industrial Revolution in North Wales*, Cardiff University Press, 1933, p. 396). In other parts of England women worked as much as sixteen hours a day (C. Day, *Economic Development in Modern Europe*, New York, 1933, p. 14). For other data on the long working hours in England from 1600 onwards, see Lipson, *Economic History of England*, vol. II, pp. 55–8 and 125–61.

[2] For the starvation wages for English weavers of both sexes in the seventeenth and eighteenth centuries, see the second volume (pp. 49–50, 62 and 125–6) of Lipson's *Economic History of England*, or A. Young's contemporary survey, *Tours in England and Wales* (No. 14 of the series of " Reprints of Scarce Tracts in Economic and Political Science," London, 1932, passim). Hauser (*Les débuts*) discusses the payment of the Lyonese silk workers.

[3] At an early date salaries began to be paid in kind in England. In 1411 at Colchester we have the first decree against the " truck system." The anonymous author of *England's Commercial Policy* (written in the first half of the fifteenth century) points out that the practice had become generally established. In 1464 a statute was drawn up which recommended that salaries should be paid " in good money " ; none the less, the truck system continued (Lipson, *Economic History*, vol. I, pp. 423–4). For the application of the same method in Italy in the fifteenth century, there is the contemporary account of G. Cambi, *Croniche*, part II, CCLXXXVIII, vol. III, p. 252, and St. Antonino, *Summa moralis*, vol. I, Chap. XVII, sec. 7. See also N. Rodolico, *Il popolo minuto*, Bologna, 1899, pp. 32–4.

[4] Lipson, *Economic History*, vol. I, p. 424.

[5] For the employment of women in agriculture and industry from 1750–1850, see Ivy Pinchbeck, *Women and the Industrial Revolution*, 1750–1850 (London, 1930). For Germany, Benaerts (*Les origines de la grande industrie allemande*, Paris, 1933, pp. 500–2) notes that the development of machinery meant the decrease in the number of women employed in industry. But Benaerts does not make it clear if the reduction was due to a general reduction in the number of hands employed, or to the substitution of male for female labour.

labour [1] was employed, even in the mining industry, so that there should be a formal justification for the low wages paid. The profits resulting from this replacement of men by women can be seen from the figures below.[2] We find a proof of the capitalistic spirit that provoked this recourse to female labour in Lord Ashley's testimony in defence of the Ten Hours Bill of 1844. " Mr. E——," he said, " a manufacturer, informed me that he employs females exclusively at his power looms ; . . .

[1] In Wales about 1830 children from six to ten years old were employed in export industries (Dodd, op. cit.). A similar state of things prevailed in the seventeenth and eighteenth centuries (Lipson, *Economic History*, vol. II, p. 61, and J. U. Nef, *The Rise of the British Coal Industry*, London, 1932, vol. II, pp. 167–8). At Lyons in the eighteenth century the Grande Fabrique employed between five and six thousand girls in the manufacture of cordage (C. Barbagallo, *L'oro e il fuoco*, Milan, 1927, p. 171).

[2] An idea of the number of women employed, but above all of the saving made possible by employing them, can be seen from the following table drawn up by Pinchbeck (op. cit., p. 193) from the information supplied by the English Factory Commission of 1833.

Women employees and salaries paid respectively to men and women employees in the cotton industry in Lancashire in 1833.

Ages.	Women employees.	Average weekly salary for women.		Average weekly salary for men.	
		s.	d.	s.	d.
0–11	155	2	4¾	2	3½
11–16	1,123	4	3	4	1¾
16–21	1,240	7	3½	10	2½
21–26	780	8	5	17	2½
26–31	295	8	7¾	20	4½
31–36	100	8	9½	22	8½
36–41	81	9	8¼	21	7¼
41–46	38	9	3½	20	3½
46–51	23	8	10	16	7¼
51–56	4	8	4½	16	4
56–61	3	6	4	13	6½
61–66	1	6	0	13	7
66–71	1	6	0	10	10

gives a decided preference to married females, especially those who have families at home dependent on them for support; they are attentive, docile, more so than unmarried females, and are compelled to use their utmost exertions to procure the necessities of life." [1]

A particular aspect of this attempt to obtain the minimum cost, and one that was confined to colonial countries, was the revival of slavery. This phenomenon can also be explained by climatic conditions under which the work had to be carried out, and which were fatal to Europeans, but if it became general in the Americas from the sixteenth century onwards,[2] it was not unknown in Italy, and Bensa tells us that in the fifteenth century in Florence slaves took the place of servants merely because they meant a reduction in household expenses.[3]

It is not irrelevant to note that if at a given moment there came to be an organized movement against slavery, this was due at once to humane motives and to the fact that European countries wished to avoid the competition of countries using slave-labour, and which could produce at lower costs. It is the capitalist spirit that urges some to use the slave as minimum means of labour. It is again the capitalist spirit, at one with religious, moral, and political agencies, that urges others to fight the use

[1] I. Pinchbeck, op. cit., p. 194.
[2] Loewenthal ("Zugtier und Sklaverei" in *Zeitschrift für Sozialforschung*, vol. II, 1933, pp. 198 sq.) has recently sought to prove that it was technical motives that led first to the introduction, then to the abolition, of slave-labour.
[3] E. Bensa, *Francesco di Marco da Prato*, Milan, 1928, p. 223.

of the slave as minimum means of labour.[1] This seems contradictory, but it is really the result of the logical fining-down of the capitalistic spirit. This fining-down, in the same way, in European countries leads the capitalist to abandon the degrading exploitation of women, children, and working men, and to turn his attention to perfecting his plant, either as soon as he perceives that the new machines can produce more in a few hours than a workman in a long working-day, or as soon as the workers' resistance to any further wage-cuts makes him consider replacing rioting men by docile machines.[2]

It would be tedious to recall the successive stages through which machinery passed before reaching its present perfection. For the purposes of the present work, however, it is useful to note that just as in early days the employer who demanded a working day of from twelve to sixteen hours had no concern for the health of the worker, the employer who to keep his industry going has to install a new machine that takes the place of ten or a hundred workers, has no concern for unemployment.

If it is true that growing rationalization has led to the adoption of this course, it is also true that once one manufacturer has embarked upon it, his threatened

[1] According to Sée (*Les origines du capitalisme*, p. 177, Eng. tr. *Modern Capitalism*, London, 1928, pp. 164–5) capitalism was one of the factors in the abolition of slavery.

[2] Lipson (op. cit., vol. I, p. 426) believes that the phenomenon appeared at the end of the fifteenth century in spite of the legal prohibitions against adopting new machines.

competitors are obliged to follow suit. The law of competition, which is the law of self-defence, makes it incumbent on all to put away any excessive concern for others, when their own existence as economic agents, and even, up to a certain point, as persons, is at stake. Driven by the law of competition, by the necessities of the struggle, by the absolute and indisputable need to obtain the minimum means, modern men sought continuously for technical improvements in their machinery, and passed from perfection to perfection, without even waiting for the machinery they had hardly introduced to wear out. Technical depreciation is the employer's constant dread, increasing his risks, magnifying his eagerness for what is more perfect. In this race for improved methods, independently of pressure from the workers, the capitalist, the descendant of the old exploiter of labour with his fifteen or sixteen hours' day at famine wages, now dreams of a minimum working day and a maximum wage, in accordance with Ford's recent declarations. The grandson of the man who recognized no holiday or day of rest in his stinking workshops, establishes the weekly rest and looks forward to a five-day week. He has realized that the hundred-and-one mediæval holidays [1] were just what he needs to give his workers in order to obtain that maximum output at

---

[1] Sombart (*Der Bourgeois*, pp. 19–20, Eng. tr. p. 19, and *Der moderne Kapitalismus*, vol. I, p. 37) sees a connection between the pre-capitalist spirit and the extraordinary number of mediæval feasts. Precise information about the number and significance of the feasts is given by us in *Le origini* (pp. 62–5).

minimum costs that his grandfather thought to obtain by driving human labour beyond its strength.

Thus the capitalistic problem of the minimum means in the labour sphere has been in existence five centuries. Such were the various provisional solutions put forward. Even without the workers' agitation, a greater perspicacity in estimating the most economical methods of production might perhaps have led the employers to take those measures that bear the name of Labour victories. In practice, they have been achieved as a result not only of workers' agitations, but also of an ever better understanding of what is profitable.[1] This could be pursued by ever more appropriate means, as gradually in the mind of man the conception of capitalistic ends grew clearer, and as gradually the adoption of such means was ever less impeded by extra-economic criteria, that is, by a pre-capitalistic mentality.

We have now, as the plan of our book demanded, briefly ascertained how the capitalist spirit impelled men to rationalization in the sphere of labour. And as this is only one aspect of rationalization, we shall proceed to examine the phenomenon from another angle, and show, no less briefly, its developments in the sphere of the

---

[1] A classic example of the concessions that might be made by employers to workers, apart from any pressure on the part of the latter, is supplied by the story of Ambrose Crowley, the owner of ironworks, who in 1690 regulated the lives of his several hundred workers by the rules laid down in his famous *Law Book*. The humane provisions made for the workers and the fact that he was the first to introduce arbiters and factory councils are typical (Lipson, *The Economic History*, vol. II, pp. 179–85). For provisions for the welfare of the workers made by French employers of the eighteenth century, see Barbagallo, *L'oro e il fuoco*, pp. 192–3.

factory. We have considered the work, let us now consider the workshop.

4. When the capitalist spirit crept for the first time into the heart of the mediæval man, it found him organizing his factors of production in a small workshop. His fixed capital was small[1]; he disposed of a minimum of hands[2]; his output was determined by orders. To obtain a reduction of costs, and hence, given the fixed maximum of prices, an increase in profit, the first promptings of the capitalist spirit were that he should anticipate demand and produce in view of hypothetical orders; he would thus be able to gain the maximum benefit from repeating the same process, the waste involved in the alternating preparation of different products would be avoided; so also would the feverish activity that followed periods when there was little or no work. It is clear that the anticipation of demand becomes the more profitable the more the actual demand increases

[1] G. Toniolo, *Dei remoti fattori della potenza economica di Firenze nel Medio Evo*, Milan, 1882, pp. 132–3.

In a footnote on p. 22 of *Le origini* we have given examples bearing on the organization of a number of mercantile establishments in the thirteenth and fourteenth centuries. These examples were taken from the writings of Bensa and Chiaudano. We must add that sums equal to those mentioned there were needed to furnish the warehouses of the Aretine merchant Simo D'Ubertino, as we can see from his account-books kept of the end of the fourteenth century, which are preserved in the archives of the lay brotherhood of Arezzo. We are bound to say that in that they relate to mercantile undertakings the value of these proofs is diminished.

[2] At Frankfort and at Ypres, a town that worked for export, as we can see from the fact that 50 per cent. of those practising a trade were textile workers, even in the fifteenth century production took place in the shop with the aid of a very small number of apprentices (Pirenne, " Les dénombrements de la population à Ypres " in *Vierteljahrschrift für Sozial- und Wirtschaftsgeschichte*, 1903, vol. I, p. 128).

in relation to the number of those who can supply it. Thus each of the latter, through the fairly high average of such demand, suffers far less risk, while the economic difference between working on order and working in anticipation of orders becomes greater. As work in anticipation of orders gradually becomes general, through increase in the actual demand and, above all, through the concentration of the increasing demand on products of small cost,[1] the craftsman's shop fills with apprentices and the number of tools must be increased. Perhaps the premises too are extended. But such enlargements make the problem of risk more serious; to reduce it, the supposititious demand must be created. It becomes necessary to attract customers, and that means to attract them away from trade rivals, and also to stimulate latent needs. The most usual method in this case is the reduction of costs, but this, as all know, whatever the period, in most cases can only be achieved by improving production as a whole. We have already seen how this end was pursued in relation to labour; we shall now see how it was pursued in relation to the factory.

According to country, industry, and situation, the anxiety to obtain low costs and increasing output led either to an increase in the number of workers in the

---

[1] It is clear that it is possible to make a candle, a handkerchief, or a pair of boots in anticipation of demand, but not, for instance, a ship. What is true to-day is, of course, still more true of the first centuries of the modern era and the last of the Middle Ages. The intelligent reader will have no difficulty in understanding the full significance of what we have said above.

workshop, and thus to transformation of the workshop itself into a manufactory on a larger scale,[1] or else the shop became a centre from which work was allotted to a certain number of workers to take home.[2] This was the extensive practice at Audenarde as early as the sixteenth century.[3] In either case, and the two are often to be found in combination, the original craftsman's workshop underwent a transformation. The owner, once the head worker, the master, step by step became the manager, and as his work came to consist more and more in co-ordination and supervision he assumed increasingly the role of an employer of labour. Save in rare cases, this metamorphosis—in view of the brevity of human life and the slowness of progress, especially in the early stages of transformation—did not show itself in one and the same person, but in a succession of several. Sometimes it would be the son of the first master weaver who, in training his apprentices, came to give less time to weaving and more to supervision. The grandson, as the size of the concern increased, might leave the looms altogether, and give himself up wholly to management and direction. It

[1] For the large number of people dependent on single employers in the textile and metallurgical industries and in commerce in the first half of the seventeenth century, see Lipson, op. cit., vol. II, p. 7. But far earlier, the craftsman's workshop must have assumed considerable proportions, if in 1395, in Essex alone, there were manufacturers able to produce 400 pieces of cloth, and a cloth-manufacturer at Barnstable could be taxed as having an output of 1,080 pieces (L. F. Salzman, *English Industries of the Middle Ages*, Oxford, new ed., 1927, p. 227).

[2] As early as the sixteenth century at Dinant a single *marchand-batteur* was providing work for upwards of a hundred persons (Pirenne, *Les marchands-batteurs de Dinant*, p. 446).

[3] Pirenne, *Note sur la fabrication des tapisseries*, art. cit., p. 335.

might be only the great grandson who would entirely lose the character of head of a textile workshop and appear simply as an employer. It was thus that the modern manufactory came into being, with an employer at its head—the descendant of weavers and the successor of men on fire with eagerness to obtain the maximum result by the means that was economically best. This aim, constant through all the variations of historical positions, counselled the discarding of all plant that had been superseded. The manufactory changed in character from day to day, and inside the division of labour came to be organized better and better.[1] Premises were enlarged, machines took the place of manual labour, new departments were added, the modern factory came into being. With time, with the widening market, the increase in potential demand, the revival of competition—bringing with it the necessity for new extensions, by which costs could be still further reduced —the factory became the great modern establishment we know, perfectly organized so as to obtain the economically best product at a cost that allows at least a momentary victory over all competition. In the matter of size, this was the goal of the capitalistically minded man in his search for a capitalistic solution of the problem of the unit of industry. This indeed had not only a dimensional aspect. There is much to be noted in regard to choice of site.

---

[1] In Birmingham in 1755 a button-manufactory employed seventy different processes (E. Lipson, *Econ. Hist. of England*).

In the pre-capitalistic period the rudimentary work-shop that had been lodged in a feudal castle or abbey was transferred to within the walls of the renascent town. Here the artisans remained for some time, fearful of exposing their apparatus to the fury of besieging forces or to enemy inroads such as they might expect outside the protection of moat and ramparts. But when the boundaries of the State spread far beyond the city walls, and the moats were no longer a barrier to enemy hordes, the artisan did not hesitate to leave the shadow of the towers for the sunlight of the suburbs, especially if, by doing so, he could escape customs and guild dues. There was also another motive that led to the transfer of manufacture to the country, and that was the possibility of engaging peasant labour at cheaper rates, either because the peasants were more ready to work for small pay, or because they were less protected by the rules of the guilds, to which they did not belong.

These considerations are nothing new. In 1560 the unknown compiler of a document discovered at Arras formulated them as follows, to justify the flight of manufactories from the town :

" A good part of those who work at a trade withdraw to the flat country and to the fields, and this not only to work at their pleasure, but also to be exempt from dues and taxes, and also to avoid the visitations and supervision to which they are subject who live in walled towns. And to this each man is the more inclined in that by nature he wishes to live in freedom, without being subject to laws or other burdens." [1]

At another period the localization of various industries was affected by considerations of climate, when it was discovered that this affected the quality of the product or the output achieved.

So long as transport was undeveloped, difficult, and costly, the capitalist gave much consideration to the position of his factory in relation to the market from which he drew his materials, to that in which he sold his goods, and to the supply of labour. Before the invention of the steam engine, industrial works had to

---

[1] Guesnon, *Inventaire chronologique des chartes de la Ville d'Arras*, p. 402, quoted by Pirenne in *Notes sur la Fabrication*, p. 335. On pp. 336–7 he gives a long passage from the said document. The accuracy and documentary precision of the information it gives on competition between urban and rural manufactories makes it worth quoting :

" What is more, besides other inconveniences, we cannot doubt that the tapestry weavers dwelling in the towns will be forced to leave them, since they cannot deliver their merchandize at the same price as the rural weavers. For we cannot be ignorant that the rural worker can make a piece of work ten or twelve *patars* cheaper than the town worker, and this for several reasons. The rural workers are not affected by tolls and dues, they are in no danger of fines if their pieces are too short or narrower than they should be. They are not prevented from working as much in inconvenient as in convenient times, they may work night as well as day. They get their lodging cheap, and also all they need to sustain their bodies and those of their servants, and they also get servant maids as they wish. Moreover, the spoilt piece of work is no less value to them than the best, for it will not be unfolded till it has been sent a hundred, two hundred, three hundred leagues. Then the buyer is cheated and will not buy any more such merchandize, and this, it is said, injures the district from which it came. But the merchant who sends it will not find fault with it, for he cares more for his own profit than for the public good, so much so that the said rural tapestry-weavers are supported by certain merchants, who ask for such merchandize so that they can have it cheap, and they have it made for them in such fashion, for it cannot be too poor for them. Thus mind, industry, and diligence are not wanted, and can make no headway, for there are higher profits to be made by indulging the other offences and frauds committed by the said rural tapestry-weavers, and especially within their workrooms."

be near waterfalls. When steam power was adopted, preference was given to coal-bearing districts. Here, in particular, metallurgical industries were located, as little by little means were found to remedy the various disadvantages of the use of mineral coal for smelting.[1] Before that, they were established near large forests, that could supply the fuel.[2] Only when the use and easy long-distance transport of electrical power placed cheap power within the reach of all did the site of the factory in relation to the source of power practically cease to be a matter of concern to the contractor. But have efforts towards economic rationalization in this direction reached their term? Assuredly, there has been much progress since the centuries when reasons of a political order tended to impede the choice of the sites that were economically best and obliged manufacturers either to remain where they could be most sure of military protection, or where the sovereign wished the royal manufactory to flourish.[3] In the struggle to achieve progressively improved conditions, it is easy to see the greater rapidity of advance from the day that society as a whole accepted

[1] Further and more detailed information on p. 12 of Birnie's *An Economic History of Europe*, London, 1933, pp. 10–11.

[2] The smelting industry was a source of so much danger to the forests that in the sixteenth and seventeenth centuries in England a vast system of legislation was framed to protect them. In the time of Elizabeth there was even a proposal to banish the iron industry from the kingdom because of the harm it was doing to the forest-lands (Lipson, *Economic History of England*, vol. II, pp. 156–8).

[3] For the different historical factors (not excluding poiitical ones) which contributed to the localization of industry, see Sombart, *Der moderne Kapitalismus*, vol. II, Chaps. XLVII and LIV.

the supremacy of the capitalist's purely economic reasoning.

In our rapid survey of past vicissitudes, we might now proceed to consider the internal organization of the factories, not only in regard to the economic features of the work done, but also in regard to supervision, control, supply of materials, environment, and lighting. It would be still easier to dwell at length on the evolution of the administrative side of industry. To do so we should have to start with the master craftsman, who may or may not make a note of his creditors,[1] pass on to the companies of Francesco di Marco da Prato and Jacques Cœur, or Lazzaro di Giovanni di Feo, with their accurate book-keeping departments,[2] or to the company of the Del Bene family, whose accountant timidly attempts to calculate industrial costs,[3] till we reached the modern firm in which the administrative side is so highly developed as to raise the question whether it would not be better to unite one factory with another so as to reduce this item of cost, making fuller use of such services, and especially of those in common. Here would be a

[1] One of them was Giubileo Carsidoni, a merchant and the owner of various brick-kilns, who lived at Sansepolcro in the fourteenth century (see A. Fanfani, *Un mercante del Trecento*, Milan, Giuffrè, 1935).

[2] E. Bensa, *Francesco di Marco da Prato*, op. cit., and R. Bouvier, *Jacques Cœur*, op. cit. So far nothing has been written on Lazzaro di Giovanni di Feo, a great Aretine merchant of the fourteenth century. But the registers preserved at Arezzo are a proof of his accurate and advanced methods of book-keeping. Some of them were kept on the double entry system. Eight commercial transactions undertaken by this merchant furnished the materials for an essay on " Costi e profitti d'un mercante del Trecento " (Outlay and profits of a fourteenth century merchant) which appeared in the *Nuova Rivista Storlica*, 1934.

[3] A. Sapori, *Una compagnia di Calimala*, op. cit., pp. 255 sq.

71

magnificent field for investigation, but one that would merely lead us to admire fresh manifestations of the now familiar capitalist spirit which, having put before men purely economic aims, leads them to achieve such aims with an ever greater surety (rationalization), by making use of means chosen and employed in accordance with purely economic criteria.

5. The process of rationalization of the factory may not perhaps appear so closely bound up with the capitalist spirit, till we remember that this process was impeded by manifold extra-economic and particularly political forces, which were overcome only through the aspirations of capitalism. Parallel to this process, we find that of the rationalization of the forms of the industrial unit from the juridical standpoint and from the standpoint of the amassing of the funds required.

The pre-capitalist period, like the capitalist, was acquainted with the private firm and with the company. When these two forms were no longer sufficient to guarantee the amassing of sufficient capital, the experiment was made of accepting deposits, the sum of which was invested in the business of the company.[1] The capitalistic era, in the teeth of considerable obstacles, created a new organism, able to amass large funds without increasing the risks of those who shared in the vast productive operations involved : this was the limited

[1] For example, the great Florentine mercantile companies, such as those of the Bardi, the Peruzzi, the Medici ; or the famous Sienese company of the Buonsignori.

company.[1] It was the ideal instrument for the capitalist, enabling him to collect immense means in small lots, and allowing the heavy burden of a risk often overwhelming in itself to be so divided up as to become almost imperceptible. The limited company, which arose where the need for abundant financial resources was greatest,[2] depersonalizes participation in economic life, and facilitates those economic enterprizes that the length of the productive cycle would make unattractive to single individuals. The action of the limited company in this sense became the more effectual in that it was soon possible to obtain the easy commercialization of shares, and also, after various vicissitudes, recognition of the limited liability of the members.[3]

It is not without reason that some have pointed to the development of the limited company as a salient feature of the capitalist system. It is useless to repeat the distinction we have already drawn on several occasions between the spirit of capitalism and the means it employs. However the question be formulated, it remains indisputable that the limited company is the ideal form, towards which, under a capitalistic régime, association for economic purposes tends, especially when the mechanization of labour has enormously increased the cost of plant. The reason for this is that the limited liability form of association allows the quota

---

[1] On the first essays in this direction in the fifteenth century, see F. Schupfer, *Il diritto delle obbligazioni*, vol. III, pp. 158-61.

[2] Lipson (*The Economic History of England*, vol. I, p. 332 ; vol. II, pp. 9 and 462) shows how this was the case in eighteenth-century England.

[3] A. Birnie, *An Economic History*, pp. 101-3.

of risk that must be personally met by each individual to be reduced to a minimum, and, on the other hand, by making use of minima of individual financial resources, it allows a maximum accumulation of capital. Moreover, since the limited company supersedes the family concern or those confined to small groups, it facilitates the elimination of personal considerations—extraeconomic considerations—in appraisement of actions connected with production. Once the capitalist spirit has taught that there must be neither recognition nor respect of extra-economic limitations to production, the consequences of this premise have developed almost automatically so as to bring about the gradual triumph of the limited company.[1] Subsequently, other goals presented themselves. After the limited company, it seemed desirable to proceed to the formation of those leviathan companies of to-day that we might call superlimited companies.

The difficulties of the market, increased by a competition that grows steadily as the capitalistic régime extends to countries previously backward in this respect, have made the problem of costs assume gigantic dimensions. Its solution seems necessarily to imply a better use of raw materials, a more scientific use of power, a more highly evolved organization of labour, easier sales, more effective finance, an increasing diminution of risk.[2] At the

[1] Cf. C. Barbagallo, op. cit., pp. 215–8.
[2] G. Masci, " Alcuni aspetti odierni dell'organizzazione e delle trasformazioni industriali " in *Nuova Collana di Economisti*, Turin, 1934, vol. VII, p. 931 ; F. Vito, *I sindacati industriali*, 2nd ed., Milan, 1932, pp. 55 sq.

point reached by the rationalization of industrial units, the solution of these problems in the capitalist economico-social system has only been possible by a process of so-called consolidation which, instead of marking the end of capitalism,[1] represents a means for its defence against the internal and external forces that hinder its further developments.[2] This phenomenon has come into being on a vast scale only in modern times, but it has historical precedents. Where such conditions as have brought it to pass to-day are to be discovered, there the perspicacious capitalist proceeded to form combines.[3] Vito's remarks, when he differentiates between ancient and modern industrial coalitions, are, from our point of view, only partially acceptable,[4] since the aim of the crudest experiments in amalgamation and that of the most scientific is always one and the same: in different historical situations to find a new means that will allow a freer course to economic action. This does not prevent our agreeing with Vito [5] that whereas in the present century the aim is to avert the evils of over-production,

---

[1] A. Ammon, *Die Hauptprobleme der Sozialierung*, Leipzig, 1920; J. B. Clark, *Essentials of Economic Theory*, New York, 1922, Chap. XXII.

[2] F. Vito, *I sindacati industriali*, p. 287; Fanfani, *Declino del capitalismo e significato del corporativismo*, art. cit.

[3] J. Strieder, *Studien zur Geschichte kapitalistischer Organizationsformen*, Munich, 1925.

Stieda, " Altere deutsche Kartelle " in *Schmollers Jahrbuch*, vol. XXXVII; A. Sayous, " Les ententes des producteurs et des commerciants en Hollande au XVII siècle " in *Mémoires de l'Académie des Sciences Morales et Politiques*, 1901; R. Piotrowski, *Cartels and Trusts, their Origins and Historical Development from the Economic and Legal Aspects*, London, 1933.

[4] F. Vito, *I sind. ind.*, pp. 94–8.

[5] Vito, " La tendenza monopolistica dei sindacati industriali " in *R.I.S.S.*, November, 1933, p. 818.

in previous centuries it was to create situations favourable to speculation.

In the labour sphere, as in that of organization, we have often come across various stages of development, a quest for a more rational solution pursued in almost opposite directions, a successive recourse to almost antithetical means. But from the centuries of the later Middle Ages up to the present day, in every field of economic life, it is not difficult to discover that, through varying vicissitudes, the goal sought by individual efforts remains fixed and unchanged.

We will say nothing of the various and often successful attempts to bring credit institutions into subordination to producing concerns as a means of facilitating financial provision for production. We shall now consider how the capitalistic man, who has solved the problems of production by solving those of labour and the organization of the industrial unit, has faced that of markets, that is to say, the complexus of problems that converge in one and must be met by the man who, having prepared his product, wishes to dispose of it. We will refrain from following the process of rationalization in all the various fields of economic life ; by confining ourselves to this one, we believe we have found a theme that will dispense us from a detailed consideration of a thousand and one minor forms of progress.

6. Before he set himself the problem of how to produce more abundantly and better, it is plain that the first

capitalistically minded man, dissatisfied with the limitations imposed on him by pre-capitalist society, first asked himself the question of what he should produce and for whom. Only when he had solved this problem would he see the necessity of finding a better means to attain the end he now saw before him : to prepare a determined product for the future consumer. In view of this, the present section should have been placed before the preceding two. We have inverted the order, as in so doing the question becomes more easily comprehensible and easier of treatment.

If the problem of sales is psychologically prior to that of production, it is also true that no sooner is an attempt made to create sales—especially if the product is not a new one, and the market in which it is to be disposed of is not virgin—than the problem immediately arises of how to improve production. Such improvement is indispensable, in every case, if new custom is to be created where previous producers seemed to have satisfied the total demand. Thus, at bottom, the problem of production comes to be identified with that of sales ; in the end the one resolves itself into the other, the first reduces itself to the second. This is what actually came to pass. When a capitalistically minded man from the fourteenth to the eighteenth century felt increased production to be imperative, in the greater number of cases he found himself faced with a market that had to be captured. There were two possibilities. Either the market was virgin and the new producer had to create the need involved, in consequence gaining the benefit of a position of momentary monopoly. Or else the market was already being exploited by others, and the new producer had to engage battle with competitors. Let us leave aside the first case, which in a short period would reduce itself to the second, and follow the economic action of the capitalistically minded man in the latter.

We have historical proofs that the neo-capitalist in the beginning sought to increase his profits by breaking all pre-capitalist rules against competition, and thus sought to gain a privileged position for himself. This he achieved either the day on which, at his own risk, he ceased to respect the generally accepted norms of conduct, or the day on which he was authorized to set them aside. However small the infraction or dispensation involved, it placed him in a particularly favourable position in relation to his competitors. In this way the neo-capitalist exploited certain favourable conditions—for example, if, sole rebel in the midst of those who respected the law, he held out special inducements to passers-by, or bribed agents to secure him customers. Or if he worked overtime, or if he could enjoy a legal monopoly, obtaining, in return for special services to reigning sovereigns, the sole right to export wool, supply cloth, work in glass, gold, or tapestry, or lend money at interest.[1] Thus and no otherwise did the first

---

[1] This was the position of the Florentine merchants in England during the Middle Ages (especially the Bardi and Peruzzi); also of the Jewish usurers bound to a city by *Capitula hebræorum*, and, in modern times, of artisans called upon to plant new industries in foreign lands.

capitalists solve the problem of the market. Thus they solved it within the State and without; thus in industry, banking, trade, transport. At one moment they profited by the weakness of the law, at another by its excellences. At one moment they evaded pre-capitalist regulations, and at another exploited them and prospered in their shadow.

In general, it was during this early period that the capitalist confused the problem of minimum cost with that of command of markets, his chief aim; even though, as a means to its realization, he was ready enough to reduce costs by the use of inferior raw materials or poor workmanship. But the time comes when he sees the question of minimum cost to be a necessary premise to command of market; it is then that we find the beginning of the series of improvements already noted, destined to rationalize both the factory and the processes of work. Of this we have already spoken. Here it is enough for us to note the attention paid by the capitalist to the problems of anticipation of consumption, to those of speculation, and to those of insurance, with a view to forestalling losses or repairing their effects.

It was partly this same object that led to the devising of advertisement as an indispensable aid in the struggle to make demand equal to supply and in the fight to capture the market. In itself, advertisement was nothing new; what was new was its scientific use on so vast a scale. In itself, it was not new if, as it seems, the walls of Pompey retain inscriptions urging prospective buyers to patronize this man or that, but it was new in relation to the Middle Ages, when the shopkeeper or merchant was not allowed to entice passers-by into his shop or warehouse, nor to bribe brokers to do so.

So long as similar prohibitions, inspired by moral and political criteria, remain in force, advertisement cannot prosper. Or, rather, it is most irrational when free competition is not allowed. Advertisement flourishes so long as the consumer has free choice of products, and the producer is left free to make them how he will, and determine their style, price, and quantity. Then, as we have said, advertisement flourishes, but it can begin to exist, as in fact, it actually began, even when such prohibitions as we have mentioned were still in force; it was then adopted by men who sought to infringe or evade them.[1] It developed enormously when it could be used, at first in sincerity, then unscrupulously, as a means to attract a customer and entice him away from others. From announcing the existence of a product, it developed into eulogy, claiming for such a product various qualities that it might or might not possess. By diverse paths, men came to use advertisement no longer to indicate the existence of products,

[1] Towards the end of the eighteenth century in France, contrary to traditional custom, certain traders attempted a form of advertisement. The immediate result was a revival of repression, for such acts were considered as an abuse by the ruling classes. A decree of 1761 declares : " Certain merchants of Paris have for some time sought to distribute among the public notices in their name announcing the sale of their stuffs or other merchandize at a price which is, they say, lower than that at which such merchandize is sold by other merchants. An offence of this nature, which is nearly always the resource of a dishonest trader, cannot be too severely punished " (R. Bigo, *La Caisse d'Escompte*, pp. 96–7).

but in order to excite wants that would shortly be satisfied with goods. The history of advertising, perhaps more than that of any other means, shows the intensity with which the capitalistically minded man pursued his end, exclusively concerned with the economic value of the means employed and despising or neglecting the moral and political prohibitions that time and again might have urged him to refrain from exciting passions, exploiting situations, using exaggeration, and so forth. What is to be said of advertisement in this respect holds good also for the new products prepared not for the satisfaction of the needs of the consumer—even of such needs as he had yet to feel—but solely the manufacturer's need for gain—a need that he tends to satisfy without asking himself whether the consumption of the new product stimulates instincts which, by extra-economic standards, it would be wrong to stimulate.

The growing need to widen the sphere of custom, or to meet competition in distant markets where other producers were established, or to reduce the costs of production in respect of that fraction accounted for by the expense of transport of raw materials from the place where they were prepared to where they were to be manufactured, brought transport problems to the fore as matters of very grave moment. To solve them meant in many cases a liberation from the influence of geographical factors on the localization of industry; nor was it of small moment to overcome political obstacles to expansion in foreign markets. Working with this end in view, the capitalistic man did his utmost to obtain the most economical mode of transport, that is, the cheapest and quickest, so that the factors of time, distance, and cost should cease to set insuperable barriers to the distribution of a product over the greatest possible number of markets. The means of transport became an integral part of production—so much so that at a given moment the final step towards the rationalization of production was taken, and the producer became directly responsible for a transport department with its own ships or its own pipe-lines. At an earlier date, in the centuries when capitalism was making its first tentative appearance, capitalists had felt the need for transport services [1] of their own, to serve their industrial, commercial, or banking enterprizes; or, better still, their own postal couriers.[2] Finally, the problem arose whether, where not only the means of transport but the roads themselves were wanting, it would not be desirable to build them. This question was answered in the affirmative by the industrialists of Upper Silesia in the nine-

---

[1] We have already noted how to improve his trade Jacques Cœur began in 1442 to build himself a large fleet for sea transport, while for land transport he used his own horses (R. Bouvier, *Jacques Cœur*, pp. 58–60). In the eighteenth century, in addition to mines and factories, the Anglesey Companies had their own ships for the transport of raw materials and products (E. Lipson, op. cit., vol. II, p. 177).

[2] In A. Frey-Schlesiger's article on " Die volkswirtschaftliche Bedeutung der habsburgischen Post im 16ten Jahrhundert " in *Vierteljahrschrift für Sozial- und Wirtschaftsgeschichte*, vol. XV, 1927, there is a reference to the first services organized by private individuals for private individuals. For the origins and rapid development of postal services, see Sombart, *Der moderne Kapitalismus*, vol. II, Chap. XXV, and Luzzatto, *Storia economica*, vol. II, pp. 44–5. Further references and a more ample bibliography will be found in Section 3 of the next chapter.

teenth century, who formed the " Social Relief Banks " for the building and maintenance of roads.[1] While a century earlier, the Duke of Bridgewater, owner of a coal-mine, financed the opening of the Manchester to Liverpool canal, when he had computed how much he could save by carrying his coal by water.[2]

This intensive action to find the best means of transport developed simultaneously with endeavours to obtain from the State the greatest freedom of transit, the best communications, the best auxiliary public services, but of this we shall speak in the following chapter.

Since the cost of transport, however much it be reduced, is none the less a cost, and hence an obstacle to the more lucrative capture of the market, the capitalist is still anxious to establish his industrial plant on what is economically the best site. His choice may be determined now by nearness of markets, whence he can draw raw materials, motive power, and man power, and now by that of the market for his finished wares. Before this problem, a thousand and one preoccupations of an extra-economic order pass into the background when they do not affect returns. Thus, for example, the capitalist in his quest for the best geographical position

---

[1] P. Benaerts, op. cit., p. 293. The Silesian industrialists could hardly fail to concern themselves with the roads, even to the point of building them themselves, if in 1844 the great furnaces of Halemba had to stop work since the bad state of the roads made it impossible to supply them with raw materials and fuel.

[2] B. and J. Hammond, *The Rise of Modern Industry*, 4th ed., London, Methuen, 1930, p. 78.

will not confine himself to his own province or his own State, but, if it is feasible, his choice may rest on foreign territory. Nor will he rule out less civilized countries, or those of different religion.

The present-day intermingling of races and peoples, with the transplantation of whole demographic groups, would not have been possible in an age in which the economic criterion had not prevailed over all others. To those who would point to the economic origin of the barbarian invasions, we reply that, in the first place, these were demographic influxes from less civilized to more civilized countries, and, in the second, their aim was booty and not rational economic exploitation. A pre-capitalist age may experience a demographic influx from civilized countries into barbarian ones, but it will have either a political or a religious aim. An economically determined influx from a civilized country into one less highly evolved is characteristic of the capitalist age in which sentimental ties and often political regulations opposed to emigration of men and capital are set aside. By this we do not mean to deny that those influxes determined by religious and political agencies did not exert a positive influence on the development of economic colonization, and hence on the extension of the market for the industries of the mother country. On the contrary, a critic might object that even in the capitalist period economic expansion is bound up with political expansion, but that critic, if he gave the matter deeper consideration, would end by admitting that it is

84

the political expansion that is subordinate to the capitalistic. It is the industries that urge the State to political colonial expansion, as a platform for economic colonial expansion. Whereas in the age of the mercantile system economic expansion, at least in the intention of its promoters, was only a means in the service of political expansion, so much so that there was no hesitation in sacrificing or curtailing the former if the latter might thereby benefit. In short, the pre-capitalist sought his new market as an auxiliary market, to which he would have recourse only when reasons of a moral and political order did not forbid. Whereas for the capitalist the new market is the region to which he will repair when he has accurately calculated the economic utility of so doing, without reference to other criteria. To avoid any misunderstanding, let us recall what we pointed out in Chapter II, and that is that we are considering the capitalist as a type, and his action not as something clearly arrested, but a tendency, an orientation.

We have sought, taking various moments of economic life, to follow through the course of centuries the process by which the capitalistically minded man has furnished himself with means that are rational in respect of his accepted ends. We have seen that a small, incipient eagerness for gain urged man towards the rationalization of his productive actions in accordance with purely economic criteria, ever more clearly determined. Let us note, as conclusion to the present chapter, that often the employment of the new means determined situations from which no retreat was possible for anyone who did not intend to end his commercial career in bankruptcy. Thus from improvement to improvement, from innovation to innovation, in the course of five or six centuries—and with especial energy in the nineteenth—a machinery has been created, the movement of which is determined by struggle against risk. We shall now see how this struggle came to involve the State itself, as chief auxiliary, and with the State finally society as a whole.

CHAPTER IV

THE STATE AND CAPITALISM

1. Necessity for capture of the State. 2. The State and Liberty.
3. The State and the Market. 4. Needs of the State.

1. WHEN the individual felt the growth within himself of capitalistic impulses and convictions, he perceived that these conflicted with the civilization in which he lived and which was defended by many public institutions. He perceived further that he could not enjoy freedom of action in accordance with his new tendencies till he had created a new civilization in which culture, the State, and public and private activities harmonized one with the other and supported one another in the work of construction. So long as the institutions of pre-capitalism, and foremost among them the State as organized for pre-capitalistic ends, remained standing, the rationalization of private activity in a capitalistic sense was doomed to ultimate failure.[1] Such rationalization could be maintained only if public life were rationalized in accordance with the same criteria, that is to say, when every State, like England in 1764, had become

---

[1] For instance, the classical instrument of capitalism, the limited liability company, could not develop freely unless the State accepted the principles of capitalism (J. Streichenberger, *Sociétés anonymes de France et d'Angleterre*, Paris, 1933, p. 34).

" a democratic republic in which commerce is God." [1]
It was to this transformation of public life that the
capitalistically minded man devoted himself, while at
the same time he completed the rationalization of private
life.

In substance, what was required was that the State
should no longer impose a special rhythm on economic
life with a view to the attainment of certain ends, but
should leave the individual free to realize his own ideals
for himself, and should confine itself to ensuring that
he should not be impeded in so doing.

This was the aspiration behind the formula presented
to the Etats Generaux of 1484 by Philippe Pot de la
Rochepot, in which he declared that the people creates
kings, who " only exist through the people." At
Dijon fifty-two years later it was proclaimed that
peoples have the right to decide their own destinies.[2]
A very curious instance of the manner in which sixteenth-
century merchants appraised the goodness of a law by
capitalistic standards, as only possible when this law was
in some way a product of their own wills, is to be found
in art. 36 of the memorial formulated by the merchants
of Antwerp, and presented by Feruffini to Philip II,
against a scheme to institute a corporation of royal
insurance agents :

[1] The Marquess of Caracciolo's judgment of England (B. Croce, *Uomini
e cose della vecchia Italia*, Bari, 1927, vol. II, p. 89) agrees substantially with
what Coke wrote in the Preface to his *Treatise* ninety-three years earlier :
" Trade is now become the Lady which in this present age is more courted
and celebrated than in any former by all the princes and potentates of
the world."

[2] H. Hauser, *La modernité du XVI siècle*, Paris, 1930, p. 70.

" The university of merchants, both those of foreign nations and those of this country, nay of this town, great and small, with one voice and by common consent, detest and abhor this ordinance and judge it as iniquitous and cruel. And it is commonly said : *vox populi vox Dei*, so that such a magistrate of brokers would be not only opposed to universal consent but also to the voice of God. If this order were profitable and good, and not to the detriment of the merchants and did no violence to freedom of negotiation, it still should not be admitted without the consent of the said merchants. But since it is evil and pestilential, as we have shown, it would be against nature and against all humanity to introduce it against the will of the said merchants." [1]

If you consider the implications of these principles in the purely economic sphere, you will have defined the final goal of capitalistic efforts in the sphere of institutions. At the beginning, the capitalistically minded sought for trivial measures of protection : since the State wished to intervene in economic life, they would be among those who profited by this inter-vention.[2] Only with increased possibility of competition was the inadequacy of this expedient felt, and, both at home and abroad, the economic agent—at first diffidently, then unconditionally—demanded freedom.[3]

[1] H. M. Robertson, op. cit., p. 79, n. 1.
[2] Luzzatto, op. cit., pp. 72–3.
[3] In Paris in 1614 freedom was demanded for the smaller trades, and a few isolated voices demanded it for the trades in general, incurring, as one would expect, the opposition of the heads of the guilds (Hauser, *Les questions*, art. cit., pp. 367—80 and 392–6). For the struggle of the English capitalists to

Thus the subordination of the State to economic activity as its protector gives place to the subordination of the State to economic activity as guarantor of its liberty in a determined system, which thereupon evolves in a capitalistic direction.[1]

This achievement, which marks the victory of capitalistic rationalization in the sphere of public institutions, finds tangible expression in the advent of parliamentary government, which identifies the ends of the State with the ends of citizens represented, ruling out the possibility that the action of the State might be informed by aims conflicting with the aims accepted by its citizens. It goes without saying that parliamentary government is not the result of economic factors only (though these contributed to it even in its earliest origins, as the story of *Magna Carta* shows), and that progress towards popular government was encouraged by the religious wars, which, as they often divided the prince from his people by reason of diversity of religion, speedily led the people to distinguish between the prince and the State, and to identify the State with the mass of citizens.

For capitalism, parliamentary government is conceived as a political instrument guaranteeing that the State

bring about the suppression of the guilds, see T. H. Marshall, " Capitalism and the Decline of the English Guilds " in *The Cambridge Historical Journal*, vol. III, n. 1, 1929, and G. Unwin, *Gilds and Companies of London*, London, 1908, Chap. XVIII.

[1] Sombart, too, maintains that there is a relation between the development of capitalism and the transformation of the State (*Der moderne Kapitalismus*, vol. I, Chap. XXI).

shall never embrace ideas not shared by members of the community, and shall never propose the realization of programmes injurious to the economic interests of the individuals who have captured the State. The one endeavour of capitalism has been to emancipate itself from ideas, or institutions based upon ideas, that impeded the economic rationalization of life. Its maximum result in the social sphere has been the parliamentary régime in a republican constitution, which makes it impossible for even the rare and feeble intervention of the head of the State to be inspired by sentiments or ideas not shared by those governed.[1] It may seem a paradox, but the most technically perfect economic realization of capitalistic civilization is the Soviet system, in which all private and public efforts have only one end: the economic rationalization of the whole of life, to the point of abolishing private property and the family,[2] and of attempting the destruction of all religious ideals that might threaten such materialistic rationalization.[3] Russia has carried the rationalizing experiment of capitalism to its highest point; she has carried it to its logical con-

[1] That what we have said of the republican, pacifist, and tolerant tendencies of capitalism is not mere imagination can be seen from the fact that such tendencies characterized the programme put forward by the mercantile party in the Low Countries and by its theorist Peter de la Cour (K. Kaser, *L'età dell' assolutismo*, p. 76). See also Luzzatto, *Storia Economica*, pp. 317–8.

[2] It is not surprising that in the dissolution of the family the Soviets should find themselves at one with one of the most representative theorists of capitalistic liberalism (Y. Guyot in the *Journal des Économistes*, 15th January, 1925).

[3] For " the economic reasons of rationalization," which are the foundation of Russian Communism, see C. B. Hoover, *La vie économique de la Russie soviétique*, Paris, 1932, pp. 9 sq. This particular point has already been illustrated in our article : *Declino del capitalismo e significato del corporativismo*.

clusion. She has taken the capitalistic ideal of the economic rationalization of life and has rendered it the ideal no longer of the individual, but of the abstract collectivity, of humanity, thus reaching the conclusion that the final obstacle to rationalization was the agent of that rationalization, man, and that this obstacle could only be removed when that same man was made the instrument of rationalization. To this end it was enough to entrust the realization of the programme no longer to the man, to the individual, who makes use of the State, but to the State which will realize the ideal entrusted to it even if the original mandatory comes to his senses.

These considerations allow us to estimate the Russian experiment at its real value, and reveal the superficiality of those who see in Communism the adversary of capitalism. It is merely its final and most highly evolved stage.[1] A system in which the basic principle is the

[1] Our own views (written in June, 1933) agree almost entirely with those expressed by Tristan d'Athayde in his book, *Fragments de sociologie chrétienne* (Paris, 1934, pp. 137–8).

" We can say without fear of error that communism is integral capitalism.

" Communism is the capitalism of the proletariat, just as capitalism was bourgeois communism.

" Communism does not deny the fundamental tenets of capitalism : it rejects only its methods. Far from rejecting the mechanization of life begun by capitalism, it sets out to complete it. Far from denying that economics are the principal basis of civilization, it maintains on the contrary that they are the *unique* basis. Communism does not react against the phenomenon of the accumulation and the concentration of capital, which Marx regarded as the real impulse behind modern capitalism ; on the contrary, in order to facilitate and control the work of concentration, it accumulates all the existing capital and concentrates the economic life into the hands of the State. Communism does not refuse consideration to commercial and industrial activities, but declares on the contrary that they are the only productive activities, the only ones capable of creating the new aristocracy of work which will take the

economic criterion cannot be the adversary of capitalism. It is the system that places other criteria above the economic that is the adversary of capitalism. Capitalism, through its agents, has fought to prevent the State from so doing; victorious, it has sought to ensure that the action of the State should be merely complementary to the free economic activity of citizens. How this came about we shall see in dealing with the State and freedom, the State and the market, and the needs of the modern State.

2. The first problem for the man who intends to act freely in a capitalistic sense is to detach the means that surround him from the concepts and ideas that make of them obstacles to his free action. In the history of European pre-capitalism these concepts are nearly all created or reinforced by religious ideas. Catholic theology and philosophy posit a religious criterion as the supreme rationalizing principle of life, even in its economic aspects, and, again, Catholic philosophy

place of the blood aristocracy of the feudal age and the moneyed aristocracy of the bourgeois period.

"Communism is therefore nothing but the logical prolongation of capitalism."

In Pirou's contribution to the volume entitled *La crisi del capitalismo* (Florence, 1933, p. 13) we read: "Denis de Rougemont maintains that communism is a privileged case of the materialist-capitalist madness, that is, that it continues capitalism rather than destroys it, carrying on the struggle in the name of a doctrine imbued with that worship of economics to which present day society sacrifices spiritual values."

Against the thesis that Communism is a continuation of capitalism, see M. Florinsky, *World Revolution and the U.S.S.R.*, New York, 1933, pp. 245–6. Some original reflections on this subject are to be found in Nicholas Berdyaev's *Christianity and Class War*, London, 1933; he holds much the same views as ourselves.

subordinates economic rationalization to political rationalization in that it relates the material well-being of the individual to the material well-being of his neighbour and subordinates purely economic well-being to individual and social well-being in the widest sense of the word. The capitalist, in his first effort to rid himself of obstacles to his action, works indirectly against religion, attacking the system of precepts that has hitherto governed the tendency of economic action. When he realizes that it is in vain to look to religion for any sanction of his mode of action, he will abandon religion as far as he himself is concerned, holding, with Turgot, that " men have no need to be metaphysicians to live honestly," [1] and will leave it to his servant who, since he cannot be expected to be an honest man—the expression is Rivarol's—had better be pious.[2]

Moreover, when Christian communities are split asunder by heresy, the capitalist attacks religion for another reason, for if diversity of creed is too acutely felt, it may create obstacles to the expansion of economic life. Even in the transition centuries the Christian merchants of Tunis felt the same need for religious indifference, and deported the Franciscan friars whose preaching threatened to destroy a peace that was highly propitious for trade.[3] Later, when religious strife spread through every country in Europe, it is easy to

[1] Turgot, "Memoire sur les prêts d'argent" in *Œuvres*, Paris, Daire, 1844, vol. I, p. 128.
[2] Groethuysen, op. cit., p. 293.
[3] B. Egidio D'Assisi, *I detti*, Brescia, 1933, p. 35 of N. Vian's Introduction.

see how each man who saw his land, his shop, his industry [1] in danger, longed for a truce and was ready to compromise in religious matters out of love of terrestrial goods. As an individual, the capitalist drew a clear distinction between the religious problem and the economic problem, inasmuch as he based his action on criteria that tended more and more to become purely economic. For him the real problem was that of preventing society, through its institutions, from guaranteeing an order based on non-capitalist principles, opposed to his own mode of action, and able to prevent its complete success. To this end the capitalist demands of the State before all else that it should free its action from the influence of religious standards—as he himself has done in his private economic life. He demands that the State should proclaim and guarantee freedom of conscience, so that his action shall no longer be fettered, directly or indirectly, by considerations of a religious order. This demand becomes more urgent as religious division grows more acute through the spread of Protestantism and its break-up into sects ; it becomes more consciously felt when even theorists like Petty and Temple point out to their contemporaries that one of the foundations of the economic prosperity of certain countries is the religious freedom they enjoy.[2] If a State that is composed of citizens of various religions embraces a certain creed,

[1] H. Levy, *Der Wirtschaftsliber.*, p. 11. Eighteenth-century documents bear witness to the extent to which religious intolerance injured the economically active classes.
[2] H. Levy, *Der Wirtschaftsliber.*, p. 7.

it immediately sets up an obstacle to the activity of those citizens who dissent from the official creed. Hence an absolute need for these to demand freedom of conscience and for the State to refrain from pursuing a particular religious course. Under pressure from these demands, in the course of centuries the institutions inspired by religion for the defence of a particular pre-capitalist system fall one by one. The law against usury is abolished, and in England usury for the first time is regulated by purely economic criteria.[1] The State no longer assists or permits the Church to intervene in questions of succession, in belated guarantee of the lawfulness of acquisitions made by the deceased. Ecclesiastical prohibitions of trade with this or that people are no longer supported by the State. The norms for the respect of honest dealing in exchanges are no longer based on the moral canons of commutative justice. Competition is no longer mitigated by aspirations towards a society based on brotherly unity. Religious holidays are no longer enforced by the State, which creates its own.[2] In a word, the civil laws tend less and less to enforce respect of ecclesiastical prescriptions, and become more and more

[1] See Tawney's Introduction to the new edition (1925) of Wilson's *Discourse on Usury*, and the pages that Ashley devotes to the problem in his well-known economic history of England.

[2] Among the earliest civil holidays created by the State in Italy are those of 19th and 26th July, instituted by the Government of Florence in memory of the victory of Cascina and the driving out of the Duke of Athens (R. Ciasca, *L'arte dei medici*, op. cit., p. 237, n. 1).

In England there was a demand for a reduction in the number of holidays as far back as the early years of the sixteenth century (G. Constant, *La réforme en Angleterre*, Paris, 1930, Eng. tr., *The Reformation in England*, London, Sheed & Ward, 1934).

independent of them. The economic action of the citizens is thus released from subjection to religious principles ; on the one hand such citizens are declared and left free to follow or not the religious creed they have individually accepted ; on the other, the laws no longer seek to defend an order towards which the State feels itself ever more alien, if not hostile, as little by little the capitalist spirit invades society. In this respect the Edict of Nantes is at once a goal and a beginning. Nor does the action of the capitalist stop here. It invades the religious sphere, and while it seeks to obtain more favourable consideration from Catholicism,[1] among the English Protestants it arouses a heterodox movement which aims at abolishing Church interference in economic affairs.[2]

We are not unaware that business men were not the only champions of toleration and freedom of conscience. Poets, like Milton, in his *Defensio pro populo anglicano*, philosophers, like Locke in his *Essay concerning Toleration*, made themselves its apologists. Voltaire, after writing the epic of the tolerant King in the *Henriade*, and his *Traité sur la Tolérance*, can boast that he had done his utmost " to contribute to the spread of the spirit of philosophy and toleration that seems characteristic of our [the eighteenth] century." (Letter to Monsieur T.)   But it must be agreed that over and above the writings of philosophers, and the lamentations of the

---

[1] Groethuysen, op. cit., pp. 253 sq.
[2] Levy, op. cit., pp. 12–13.

persecuted, " the most effectual agent of all in promoting the new ideal was the development of trade resulting from the rise of the middle class. For what possible reason could a trader concern himself with the religious faith of those with whom he traded ? For him the one and supreme God is utility, whose earthly manifestation is money ; that is enough. To Voltaire the London Stock Exchange seems almost a sacred spot, and certainly more respectable than many courts. There, he remarks acutely, men of all religions treat with one another without asking in whom or in what they believe *et ne donnent le nom d'infidèles qu'à ceux qui font banqueroute.*" [1] Inevitably, the man who has made the increase of his trade and the rationalization of his business his end in life could not accept a restriction of his activity that was unjustified from the economic standpoint. Therefore it is the capitalist who, as more directly concerned, more or less noisily proclaims his spirit of toleration and his aspiration towards religious liberty, even though it was not he himself who inspired the doctrinaires.[2]

When capitalists had won this victory, and established the principle of secularism, they had led the State to take the first decisive step towards a capitalistic rationalization of society. The State, no longer guardian of religious ends as the supreme ends of society, became the guardian of its own, political ends, and sought to

---

[1] A. Gerbi, *La politica del Settecento*, Bari, 1927, p. 115. For the struggle for toleration in France, see Mornet, op. cit., p. 39 ; for both France and England, see T. Buckle, *History of Civilization in England.*
[2] Groethuysen, op. cit., pp. ix–x of the Preface.

subordinate economic actions to these. Practically, capitalistic rationalization was still rendered impossible and impeded precisely because the State sought another rationalization, a political rationalization, often opposed to economic rationalization and always distinct from it. This implied a disbelief in purely economic criteria as the principles of rational order. It meant, moreover, that such order was to be realized in the interests of a collectivity, envisaged not as a total of individuals, but as a higher body distinct from that total. As a result of this ideal, the brief parenthesis of the sixteenth century, when it seemed that economic life, having thrown off religious bonds, was henceforth free, was followed by a period of constriction, which, if it can boast the revocation of the Edict of Nantes in the religious field, in that of politics marks the triumph of absolutism, and in economics coincides with the period known as that of mercantilism.[1] The triumph of a political criterion as the moderator of the whole of life is, we believe, the explanation of that return to the old order that is to be found in the seventeenth century as opposed to the sixteenth.[2] In the history of Europe from the sixteenth to the eighteenth century, this ideal

---

[1] Kaser, *L'età del' assolutismo*, p. 24.

[2] Hauser, *La modernité*, p. 12. In the industrial world we find a typical example of reaction of this kind. In their regulations for 1554 the silk workers of Lyons look forward to complete freedom of work (" *Pas de stage d'apprendissage, ni de compagnonnage, de restriction dans le nombre de métiers et celui des apprentis : les maîtres emploient qui leur plaît* ") which they begin to limit again from the end of the sixteenth century onwards. E. Pariset, *Histoire de la fabrique lyonnaise, Etude sur le régime social et économique de l'industrie de la soie à Lyon depuis le XVI siècle*, Lyon, 1901.

implied the absence of civil liberty in the modern sense, but it implied also the capitalist struggle to achieve it. They would achieve it now by a temporary privilege, now by unpunished infraction, and finally as an incontestable guarantee of freedom of economic action without necessity to render account to any but themselves, and with no obstacle to action other than their own detriment. The capitalistic man realized that this achievement was indispensable to the economic rationalization of life ; to have failed to attain it would have revealed the utter uselessness of the attainment of religious liberty.[1] For under such circumstances economic life, though no longer controlled in the name of divine religion, would have been controlled by political ends, that is, by a religion of the State, which was often no less hostile to capitalistic ends than the religion of a divinity. Thus the efforts of the capitalist against absolutism—assisted, whether consciously or no, by the new philosophers and the forerunners of the economists—acquires its full significance. And thus the complaints of Englishmen of the seventeenth century against monopolies [2] are closely connected with the actions of

[1] Kaser (*L'età dell' assol.*, pp. 304–5) draws attention to the close connection between freedom of conscience and civil liberty, both political and economic.
[2] Lipson, op. cit., vol. III, pp. 357 sq. When judgment was given about a soap patent in 1656 it is declared that " common and vulgar judgments . . . condemn them before they understand them, as being contrary to the liberty of the subject and the freedom of trade " (p. 365). But similar arguments against monopolies had already been adopted in a bill presented to the House of Commons in 1604, urging that monopolies should be abolished on the grounds that " all free subjects are born inheritable . . . to the free exercise of their industry " while " it is against the natural right and liberty of the

the manufacturers who struggled to free France from the domination of the guilds, with the struggle of the German industrialists to obtain the passing of a law on vocational freedom in 1869,[1] and with the resolutions of the Manchester School in favour of free trade.

Abolition of monopolies, the struggle against the guilds, the removal of the fetters on industry, war on customs barriers—such are the more notable directions in which the capitalistically minded man has worked from the sixteenth century to our own,[2] till he comes to declare that in the production, circulation, and distribution of wealth there can be no higher interest than his own, and that no one better than the interested party can reach the desired goal. The new exponents of political economy banish all doubt as to the lawfulness of such free action, and declare with the Abbé Baudeau that " all profit is just where there is full freedom."

The efforts of theorists and practical exponents of this attitude meet with their first success in the suppression of the corporations,[3] decreed by many States after 1770, following the example of Leopold of Tuscany.

---

subjects of England to restrain it into the hands of some few as now it is " (I, p. 498). For protests previous to 1597 and 1601, see J. Mazzei, *Politica economica internazionale inglese prima di Adamo Smith* (Milan, 1924, p. 52).

[1] P. Benaerts, op. cit., Chap. XV.

[2] For the neo-capitalists' movement in the direction of freedom in the sixteenth century, see Pirenne, *Les périodes*, p. 21. On the movement in general towards economic freedom, see C. Barbagallo, *L'oro e il fuoco*, pp. 179 sq. In the seventeenth century the Swiss bourgeois vigorously affirmed their faith in the benefits of commercial freedom (B. Biucchi, *Tendenze liberistiche nella storia economica della Svizzera* in *R.I.S.S.*, July, 1934).

[3] See R. Ciasca, " Le ragioni della decadenza delle corporazioni medievali " in *Vita e Pensiero*, May, 1934, pp. 275–87.

In 1769 they also obtained not only the suppression of the French East India Company, but a declaration of free trade between the colonies and the mother country. Nineteen years later, the example of France was followed by Holland, who suppressed her own India Company, while in the meantime Spain authorized her colonies to trade with one another, the ports of the French colonies were flung open to foreign ships, and the Treaty of Eden provided for a policy of commercial liberalism between France and England even in time of war.[1] These were the early successes obtained by the champions of economic liberalism in the eighteenth century, but they were sufficient to foreshadow the inevitable course of the world towards those ends that, achieved by the more highly evolved European countries during the nineteenth century, would create a politico-economic system fully in harmony with the needs of capitalism; so much so that the fate of capitalism would be compromised as soon as the loyalty of States to a policy of economic liberalism became a myth.[2]

The crown of the building, the guarantee of its stability, are political liberties, through which the citizen co-operates in forming the will of the State, and the State undertakes as its end the realization of the

---

[1] Mazzei (*Polit. ec. inter.*, Chap. XII) has exemplified the significance of the economically liberal Treaty of Eden, which has been studied by F. Dumas (*Etude sur le traité de commerce de 1786 entre la France et l'Angleterre*, Toulon, 1904).

[2] Cabiati (*Crisi del liberalismo o errori d'uomini ?* Turin, 1934, pp. 200–2) maintains that there is a close connection between capitalism and liberalism, so much so that now that liberalism is being abandoned, capitalism must collapse.

order approved by the groups of citizens in power. "The new parliaments," writes Barbagallo, "carry on to the stage of history the more numerous classes possessed of liquid wealth—traders, industrialists, bankers, and, lastly, workers—who in the end force public affairs into a direction conformable to their interests, which are all bound up with the fact of industrial production. That is why England, already a constitutional monarchy in the eighteenth century, is the first to enter the realm of large-scale machine industry. That is why the triumph of the latter begins in France with the fall of the Bourbon monarchy and the advent of the so-called July monarchy (1830), which marked the rise to power of the upper middle classes. And finally, that is why in Germany big industry was born after the State had become parliamentary, that is, after 1870 ; this was also the case in Italy, Japan, Belgium, etc."[1]

In the age that has seen the end of the century-long struggle between the private forces of capitalism, which remain victorious, and the public forces of pre-capitalism, which are overpowered, it is clear that the order to be defended by the new State is a capitalistic order. To this the laws bear witness. In spite of the persistence of a certain opposition, they are passed to safeguard an individualistic conception of property and the complete autonomy of the individual in economic matters, and to defend economic freedom even against the power of the

[1] Barbagallo, *L'oro e il fuoco*, p. 203. See the same writer's *Le origini della grande industria contemporanea*, Venice, 1929–30, vol. I, p. 77.

State itself. The power of the State to discipline production and trade, at home and abroad, is restricted; so also is its capacity to demand a quota of the revenues from private estates. Some of these laws anticipated the advent of capitalism to power, and many of them were concessions made by the old State, when the last sovereigns of the *ancien régime* were " enlightened " by the new propositions of eighteenth-century theorists. Most follow the triumph of capitalism; they are then opposed by the small remaining sections of extreme Conservatives, who, in the middle of the nineteenth century, pant for the restoration of institutions of which the only *raison d'être* was the defence of a non-capitalistic order. A history of economic and civil legislation from the sixteenth to the nineteenth century, from the age in which we find groups of capitalistically minded individuals to the age when these groups have become whole nations, would show the chronological succession, from day to day, of such acts as we have mentioned. The logical plan of the present work, which has allowed us the better to arrange our data and co-ordinate processes, has prevented us from making more than the most fleeting reference to facts of this kind. But the conclusions of such a detailed history would confirm our own, in which we have taken full account of political, religious, economic, and theoretical developments. All converge towards one end, because all are informed by one idea : to build up a social organization not at variance with the ideals that, from the fifteenth to sixteenth cen-

104

turies onwards, were those of an ever increasing number of men, who in the nineteenth century became the guides of humanity.

3. In actual fact, capitalism received considerable encouragement from the State in various fields; at first during the mercantile period, when it can hardly have expected it; then during the liberal period, as a result of its direct pressure.

The absolute State encouraged the early expansion of capitalism. Probably it did so accidentally, in seeking the realization of its own ideals—unless it can be proved that capitalists were able to direct the aims of the mercantile State to further their own interests. However this may be, incipient capitalistic undertakings received not a few privileges from the absolute monarchs. At one moment it would be a monopoly, a source of considerable profit to the beneficiaries, as Lipson has shown in respect of England.[1] At another it would be direct encouragement through purchases,[2] large subsidies.[3] Or else the subjects of the sovereign would be obliged to purchase certain manufactured articles.

Where the State adopted this benevolent attitude,

---

[1] Lipson, op. cit., vol. III, pp. 362 sq.

[2] P. Boissonnade, Le socialisme d'Etat, pp. 29–30. Between 1515 and 1553 Francis I spent 20,000 lire on purchasing lace from the same merchant; in eight years the same king spent 80,000 lire on silk. In 1514 alone 27,270 lire were spent on copper and pewter and 58,000 on gold work.

[3] In Austria by 1785 the State had already granted 680,000 gulders to employers as subsidies. And Russia forces the subjects to buy the manufactured goods (J. Kulischer, " La grande industrie aux XVII et XVIII siècles " in Annales d'Histoire Economique et Sociale, 1931, pp. 18–19).

in the course of a few years manufactories increased in number and capacity. Frederick the Great of Prussia, who founded Prussian industry, saw the number of manufactories increase to 1,902 ; the 2,000 workers employed in 1765 had become 16,500 twenty years later. Under Catherine II of Russia, the 948 industrial concerns existing in 1762 had become 2,948 in 1796.[1] Such were the outstanding results witnessed by the eighteenth-century successors of sovereigns who, in other countries and when the times were not so ripe, had preceded them in unsuccessful attempts of the same nature.[2]

The absolute State encouraged early capitalism in another manner by placing cheap labour at its service. Charles VII granted Jacques Cœur the privilege of pressing idlers and vagabonds to serve on his ships.[3] His successors authorized tapestry-weavers, glass blowers and pottery workers to employ children from the foundling hospitals.[4] The King of Prussia gave a certain Hirsch the Potsdam orphans to work at making velvet.[5] And in Prussia and Austria even the soldiers worked for industry. Soldiers on leave were sent to the manufactories ; those in barracks carded and wove wool,

[1] Kulischer, art. cit., pp. 12–14.
[2] At Naples King Charles II, attempted to establish a woollen industry (R. Caggese, *Roberto d'Angiò e i suoi tempi*, Florence, 1922–30, vol. I, p. 77). In England Edward III inaugurated industrial protectionism (Lipson, op. cit., vol. I, p. 400). In the same century Louis XI founded silk factories at Lyons and Tours.
[3] J. Bouvier, *Jacques Cœur*, p. 61.
[4] P. Boissonnade, *Le socialisme d'Etat*, pp. 212 and 295.
[5] Hintze-Schmoller, " Die preussische Seidenindustrie im 18 Jahrhundert " in *Acta Borussica*, vol. I, n. 146.

and at Bratislava five regiments quartered in the town spun cotton for a local contractor.

All these measures, and the many others mentioned in any economic history of the period,[1] encouraged the development of capitalist industry, establishing it in an honourable position, supplying it with financial resources, easing its burdens, and generally facilitating its expansion. But there is also another way in which the modern State has accelerated the victorious advance of capitalism. The formation of national political unities, that began with the dawn of the modern era, favoured the widening of markets and paved the way for experiments in rationalization that would otherwise have been impossible. Capitalism derived still greater advantages from being able to expand over the wide territories of a State in which the feudal substructures were demolished one by one.[2] This advantage reached a maximum whenever a single language prevailed throughout the whole of the State, and the same laws held good for a vast territory. The reader who has followed our argument that capitalism necessarily demands a vast market, will realize that it is not imprudent to hold that the action

[1] J. M. Kulischer (*Allgemeine Wirtschaftsgeschichte des Mittelalters und der Neuzeit*, Munich, 1928, vol. II, Chap. II) discusses the help given by the State to the development of big industry. On the importance of the mercantile policy of the State of the seventeenth and eighteenth centuries for the development of capitalism, see Boissonnade's *Colbert* (Paris, 1932) and *Le socialisme d'Etat* and Kulischer's valuable study already quoted (*La grande industrie*).

[2] It required the Constituent Assembly to free the French market from internal customs dues. For the influence of the increase of these obstacles on the economic life of an eighteenth-century State, see R. Ciasca, *Aspetti della società e dell' economia del Regno di Napoli nel secolo XVIII*, art. cit., p. 650.

of the mercantile period to enlarge the State and increase its authority at the expense of local autonomies, unconsciously did much to favour the formation of the vast market required for capitalistic expansion.

Experiments of rationalization could be carried out to the more advantage, the greater the security of existence and circulation for persons and goods. This security reached its maximum, as compared with that of mediæval society, with the establishment of the absolute State of the seventeenth and eighteenth centuries, while it found a guarantee against arbitrary acts on the part of the sovereigns themselves with the advent of the constitutional régime. A security in perfect consonance with the requirements of capitalism was only obtained when the norms that determined it were established by representatives of capitalism itself, but this does not mean that in the pre-capitalistic period capitalism did not find greater security under absolutism than in the States of the Middle Ages. The absolute monarchies, even though their premises might conflict with those of capitalism, favoured it in this and other respects.

Moreover, we must not forget that even the absolute State did not disdain to surround itself with economic councils. Such were established in the Kingdom of Naples by Charles de Bourbon, in Piedmont by Victor Amedeo,[1] in France by first Louis XI[2] and later by

---

[1] R. Ciasca, *Aspetti della società e dell' economia del Regno di Napoli nel secolo XVIII*, art. cit., p. 650.

[2] In 1475 Louis XI called together the bourgeois and merchants of Paris, to counsel him on the great *Ordonnance*, which appeared in 1479. In 1482 he

Colbert, who founded his *Conseil du Commerce* in 1664. Similar councils sprang up in Switzerland side by side with aristocratic Governments (the *Commerzienrath, Kaufmännisches Direktorium*, of the eighteenth century), while as early as 1599 the active and vigilant Chamber of Commerce of Marseilles had its own ambassadors at the French Court.[1]

In yet another and undeniably effective manner the State acted in favour of capitalism and the unity of the national market in establishing uniformity of law. This was attempted by Colbert, by his ordinances on civil proceedings (1667) and criminal proceedings (1670), and above all by his two Codes, the Commercial Code of 1673 and the Navigation Code of 1681. Nearly a century later the Austria of Joseph II took similar measures (the *Strafgesetzbuch* of 1787, the *Allgemeines bürgerliches Gesetzbuch* of 1788), and the Prussia of Frederick II did likewise (*Das allgemeine preussische Landsrecht*, 1794). In this way one of the gravest obstacles to the expansion of economic life was removed.

Another means of unifying the market is the establishment of uniform weights and measures. The absolute States made a certain progress in this direction, and sometimes succeeded in abolishing or reducing the inconveniences of local systems of weights and measures.

called a similar assembly to discuss the organization of the merchant fleet (Boissonnade, op. cit., p. 18).

[1] Fournier, " La Chambre de commerce de Marseille et ses représentants à Paris " in *Études Historiques et Documents Inédits*, Marseilles, 1920.

The bourgeois spirit, regardless of tradition, which had maybe withheld the absolute rulers from such reforms, was not satisfied with what had been achieved and wished to go further. Through its impulse, after the Convention had unified weights and measures throughout France, the attempt was made to extend the metric decimal system to the whole world. In the money sphere attempts, no less inspired by capitalistic interests, were made to form monetary unions.

It is possible that the various States entered upon these courses for political and not for economic ends, but they were encouraged to pursue them by the eagerness of the capitalist groups for rationalization. These saw in such attempts on the part of the mercantile and liberal State respectively effectual means of creating a huge market in which, given free competition, economic rationalization would tend to reduce risk to a minimum.

In speaking of State action—at first merely exploited, then maintained by capitalism—to widen the market, we cannot pass over the importance assumed by improved communications. To this end Louis XIV created the State corporation of *Ingénieurs des Ponts et Chaussées*, while in the seventeenth century, to supply deficiencies, the canals of the Seine and Loire and those of Toulouse and Orleans were opened. It may be objected that these measures, like the improvement of the roads in England at the end of the eighteenth and beginning of the nineteenth century, were not always governed by economic aims [1]; it may be asserted that purely military considerations led to a revival of the Roman passion for fine roads in the Napoleonic era.[2] But it cannot be denied that the pressure of the commercial classes contributed not a little to the solution of the grave and pressing problem of communications.[3]

When the problem of the roads was solved, thanks to technical inventions that facilitated their sound construction and maintenance, much still remained to do. It was necessary to organize the means of transport, and, coming to the assistance of its citizens, the State has either subsidized such private means or created its own. Thus we find first the postal and courier services [4]; then navigation lines, railways, and motor transport, which is now gaining primacy over earlier systems. For the transport of news, in competition with earlier services and completing them, the telegraph, telephone, and wireless are developed. The obstacles interposed by the sea and vast distances are overcome by submarine

---

[1] J. and B. Hammond, *The Rise of Modern Industry*, op. cit., pp 70–6, and J. F. Rees, *A Survey of Economic Development*, London, 1933, pp. 173–8.

[2] E. Tarlé, *Le blocus continental et le royaume d'Italie*, Paris, 1928, pp. 51–5.

[3] This has been shown by Borlandi to be true of the Italy of the eighteenth century (*Il problema delle comunicazioni nel secolo XVIII nei suoi rapporti col Risorgimento italiano*, Pavia, 1932).

[4] For the beginnings of the postal service, see F. Ohmann, *Die Anfänge des Postwesens und die Taxis*, Leipzig, 1909; A. Frey-Schlesinger, *Die Volkswirtschaftliche Bedeutung*, op. cit., p. 464; G. Luzzatto, op. cit., pp. 44–5; Sombart, *Der moderne Kapitalismus*, vol. II, Chap. XXV; A. Schulte, *Die Geschichte des mittel. Handels und Verkehrs*, Leipzig, 1900, vol. I, pp. 500–10; E. Motta, " Un regolamento postale milanese del 1535–6 " in *Archivio Storico Lombardo*, 1906, vol. II, pp. 424 sq.; L. Belgrano, " La posta a Genova " in *Archivio Storico Italiano*, 1868, Series 3, vol. III, Pt. i, pp. 61 sq. Boissonnade (op. cit., pp. 59–60) refers briefly to the French post in the fifteenth century.

cables and wireless telephony. Such services, and innumerable others that complete them, bring places close together, turn the world into a single city, reduce the difficulties of transport problems, and widen the market. As the agency and means of this expansion, we find the State at first dominated by a non-capitalistic conception, but none the less serving the interests of capitalism, and later at the disposal of triumphant capitalism. In the colonial sphere also its action unconsciously produces various combinations of circumstances propitious to capitalism,[1] till capitalism demands that colonial conquests shall have this significance and no other : to procure markets for the mother country, and to acquire territory that shall complete it economically. The political aim is at first exploited as an occasion for economic advantage ; then it becomes a definite means for the achievement of economic ends. Always, the State is the instrument, consciously so only with the passing of time, of the capitalistic organization of the world. To complete this, at least as regards the market, the State must place its diplomats at the service of economic life, and these must draw up treaties or live abroad to watch over the economic interests of their country. The State must fetter its own autonomy by customs unions for the sole reason that these may be of advantage to the economic system. And it will be ready

---

[1] As a typical instance of the impetus given by capitalism to the conquest of colonies, we may quote Madagascar, which, seized by merchants, was retained by France contrary to the plans of the French Government (H. Froidevaux, " Le commerce français à Madagascar " in *Viert. für Sozial- und Wirtschaftsgeschichte*, 1905, pp. 41–3).

to abandon any tariff policy if at a given moment of history a régime of absolute freedom in international trade becomes the supreme desire of the business men and theorists of capitalism.

4. By the very fact of its needs, the modern State was a means, at first unconsciously, then consciously, for the realization of capitalistic ends. Such needs assumed such outward expression as to become cause and encouragement to capitalistic expansion, and particularly inasmuch as they allowed demand to crystallize in a market of which the scale and permanence were such as to guarantee the most hazardous experiments in rationalization. Such experiments did not appear so hazardous, through the sole fact of a multiplication of public needs, which revealed themselves on a scale previously unknown from the moment an absolute conception of the State endowed it with functions that were unthinkable in the Middle Ages. Nor when this conception declined did such needs decline with it. Indeed, they were replaced by others, but these others were no less, nor did they call for fewer workers or a smaller mass of products to supply them.

Needs of defence led to a great increase in military industries, so much so that when, in early days, the efforts of private enterprize proved inadequate, the State had either to take over the preparation of arms and powder,[1]

---

[1] Such was the policy of the Valois kings in the opening years of the sixteenth century (P. Boissonnade, *Le socialisme d'Etat*, pp. 51–8).

or to form companies which, like the Russo-Prussian, supplied cloth for uniforms, caring little if at the same time they made considerable profits.[1] When the State had recourse wholly to private persons, it enabled these to make their fortunes simply from orders in respect of armaments. Between 1601 and 1607 the French State spent 12,000,000 fr., and 4,000,000 in 1639 alone. Nor did this fervour decrease with change of ministers. Sully, Richelieu, Mazarin, are alike in such expenditure, and only the Minister of Finance, Bullion, ventures to note that artillery " devours finance." [2]

Such needs of a military nature did not cease with the end of the war period that is a special feature of the age of absolutism.[3] The need to be prepared for defence was not ended, nor were the wars. Apart from the Napoleonic wars, during the course of the nineteenth century there were always enough for military needs to exercise a perceptible and beneficial influence on industrial activity.[4] On the other hand, the professional armies of absolutism were replaced by conscripts. And if in the most capitalistic countries in the world, Great Britain and the United States, enlistment became voluntary, the reasons for this are in nothing contrary to capitalist mentality. The new armies withdrew citizens

---

[1] Kaser, op. cit., p. 27.

[2] Boissonnade, op. cit., pp. 205–6.

[3] Sombart, *Krieg und Kapitalismus*, Munich, 1912, and *Der moderne Kapitalismus*, vol. I, Chap. XXII.

[4] Even the tiny Austro-Piedmontese war of 1848–9 " made the fortunes of the army contractors " (Bachi, *L'economia e la finanza delle prime guerre per l'indipendenza d'Italia*, Rome, 1930, p. 32, n. 2).

from productive activity for a few months only, while, owing to the vast number and constant succession of those called to the colours, they led to a greatly increased need for material. This continuous demand for clothing, food supplies, arms, and equipment, which can be estimated in advance, renders the organization of industry more supple, rationalization more profitable, and production for future demand less risky. These military needs bring all the more advantage to capitalism, in that the most capitalistic industries are those connected with defence, while the maintenance of strong, numerous, and powerful armies not seldom finds champions in groups deeply involved in the heavy industries. Capitalism is opposed to war so long as war means an interruption of trade and destroys international balance, but it is not opposed to armaments which allow the persistence of a large proportion of market-demand and guarantee to this demand a certain stability ; above all, capitalism knows how to profit by war to create fresh scope for itself.[1]

What we have said of the needs of defence may be repeated in respect of the needs involved by public works, the execution of which profits capitalism in various ways. It renders transit less difficult, when such

[1] For the documents relating to Italian industry and the World War, see L. Einaudi, *La condotta economica e gli effetti sociali della guerra italiana,* Bari, 1933, Chaps. II and III, and V. Franchini, *La mobilitazione industriale dell'Italia in guerra, contributo alla storia economica della guerra 1915–1918,* Rome, 1932.

For documents relating to the other belligerent nations, see the different volumes of the *Storia economica e sociale della guerra mondiale,* published by the Carnegie Foundation.

works, as in many cases, concern the creation and maintenance of communications. It absorbs a certain and fairly constant quantity of products prepared by private industry. In years of crisis it forms a real god-send to those who have their warehouses packed with unsold goods, and who, as private demand diminishes or disappears, would have to close down their works at grave loss. The State, by carrying out public works in a capitalist-liberal régime, lessens the risks of producers, and almost plays the part of an insurance system.

We must not forget how greatly capitalist expansion has benefited by the role of the State in public education.[1] In so far as an increased demand for products on the market is concerned, this function plays a small, even negligible part ; on the other hand, it facilitates business inasmuch as it means the spread of culture, indispensable for economic progress. This is so true that it was precisely the commercial classes who saw the need to increase education, and, before the State intervened to this end, they themselves promoted its diffusion.[2]

To fulfil these functions, and others that we have not mentioned, the State has had an increasing need of financial resources. Does it therefore work against capitalism by drawing off funds ? Having noted that in

[1] Todd (*Industry and Society*, op. cit., pp. 434 sq.) indicates the relations between the development of culture and industrial progress. Sombart also has some interesting remarks to make about the same problem.

[2] Skilful researches have enabled L. Mazoyer to prove this in connection with a limited field of French territory (Mazoyer, " Rénovation intellectuelle et problèmes sociaux : la bourgeoisie du Gard et l'instruction au début de la monarchie de Juillet " in *Annales d'Histoire Economique et Sociale*, January, 1934, pp. 20–39). See also Todd, op. cit., p. 448.

the period of early capitalism the State was the bankers' best client and enlarged their scope,[1] we consider that the question should be divided into two sections, and a distinction drawn between the funds absorbed by taxes and levies and those absorbed by loans. The former is, at bottom, merely an equivalent of services rendered, and from which capitalism derives advantages. The second corresponds also to services rendered, but on occasion it is also of great advantage to capitalism in absorbing funds that may be lying idle. Anyone can see from this that the function of the extraordinary financial needs of the State becomes that of compensating and regularizing the demand for money on the market. This is true when the loan is not compulsory. If it were a case of a forced loan, it would be merely the equivalent of a service without the advantages offered by a free loan. It may be objected that these remarks leave no room for waste, misuse, or bad administration. Precisely. We presuppose that in a capitalistic régime the State tends to regulate public finance in accordance with economic rather than political criteria, and that at bottom it fulfils those economic functions that private individuals would not be able to compass. It was because this was not always the case that the capitalist has sought to capture the State and withdraw its activity from the influence of ideals conflicting with capitalistic ideals. Where there is dissipation of resources, in the

[1] P. Sagnac, " Le crédit de l'Etat et les banquiers à la fin du XVII et au commencement du XVIII siècle " in *Revue d'Histoire Moderne*, vol. X, 1908, and Sée, *Les origines du capitalisme*, op. cit., pp. 92–3 (Eng. tr., pp. 81–2).

economic sense, we must distinguish whether this dissipation is accidental or deliberate. In the first case it may be said that there has been an error in calculation, such as might be perpetrated by the most wary capitalist. The second would mean that the government of the State was dominated by a conception that did not coincide with the capitalistic conception : that is to say, that capitalism had either failed to capture or had lost its control of the State.

In the full triumph of capitalism, therefore, the State has a definite function as a means for the attainment of the ends that capitalist conviction sets before man. We have briefly noted how it fulfils this function as guarantor of freedom and by facilitating economic life. We have also seen how capitalistically minded men have led it to fulfil this function.

We have now concluded our survey of the public and private instruments of capitalism. We hope to have shown how they do not constitute the essence of the system, and that therefore it is a mistake to characterize the system in terms of such instruments, forgetting that they have always existed to a greater or less degree, and that with the advent of the new spirit they merely changed their function. Of this change of function we might speak, indeed, as a characteristic feature of capitalism.

CHAPTER V

CATHOLICISM AND CAPITALISM

1. Social ethics of Catholicism. 2. Catholic ideals and capitalist ideals. 3. Catholic actions and the progress of capitalism.

1. THE Catholic ideal of economic life finds condensed expression in the principles of the Gospels,[1] which were elaborated successively by St. Paul, the Fathers, and the Doctors [2] till, in the age of the *Summae* and of Scholasticism, St. Thomas Aquinas, prince of Catholic philosophers, grafted Catholic principles on to the old, all but forgotten, trunk of Aristotelianism, scattering through his works a series of maxims, which, taken as a whole, enable us to attain an accurate and complete vision of economic life according to Catholic ideals.

Our choice of a thirteenth-century Doctor will in no wise prevent us from embracing either the age that

---

[1] A. Lugan, *L'Evangile et les biens terrestres*, Paris, Spes, 1920.

[2] For Christian teaching on wealth, cf. G. Boucaud, *St. Grégoire le Grand et la notion chrétienne de la richesse*, Paris, Gabalda, 1912; V. Brants, *L'Economie politique au Moyen Age*, Louvain, Peeters, 1895; W. Endemann, *Studien in der romanischkanonistichen Wirtschafts- und Rechtslehre bis gegen Ende des siebzehnten Jahrhunderts*, Berlin, Guttentag, 1874; R. Gonnard, *Histoire des doctrines économiques*, Paris, Valois, 1930; G. O'Brien, *An Essay on Mediæval Economic Teaching*, op. cit.; E. Troeltsch, *Die Soziallehren der christlichen Kirchen und Gruppen*, op. cit.; M. Vignes, " Les doctrines économiques et morales de Saint Bernard sur la richesse et le travail " in *Revue d'histoire économique et sociale*, 1928; A. Brucculeri, Il pensiero sociale di S. Agostino, Rome, " *La Civiltá Cattolica*," 1932. These are the principal works, and contain exhaustive bibliographical information.

119

preceded or the age that followed. St. Thomas gave systematic expression to the Catholic ideas professed before his time; he is the source, sometimes in germ, but often *in extenso*, of those professed after him. We therefore find it most convenient to take his formulation of economic ethics, inasmuch as it is the most systematic and the widest in scope; it gives us greater surety of exact interpretation of Catholic thought, inasmuch as the Church recognizes it as having the greatest authority. Under very different circumstances, Leo XIII, the Social Catholics of the last century, Pius XI, and contemporary students of economic ethics,[1] appeal precisely to the principles of St. Thomas. These principles remain constant. The vicissitudes of history have led the Church and her theorists to interpret their bearing upon contingent circumstances,[2] but into these interpretations we need not enter; we have mentioned them in proof of the undisputed authority of St. Thomas as exponent of Catholic teaching.

Catholic doctrine does not divide practical life into water-tight compartments. The idea of God and the idea of man, who is conceived as a creature struggling to attain the prize of eternal happiness, penetrate all others. At every moment, from birth to death, man is

[1] The following are worthy of note in view of the depths and value of their work : O. Nell-Breuning (*Grundzüge der Börsenmoral*, Freiburg im Breisgau, Herder, 1928) ; O. Schilling (*Katholische Sozialethik*, Munich, Hueber, 1929) ; P. Tischleder and H. Weber (*Handbuch der Sozialethik*, vol. I, *Wirtschafts-ethik*, Essen, Baedeker Verlag, 1931).

[2] Manuel Rocha, in *Travail et salaire à travers la Scolastique* (Paris, Desclée, 1933) has shown the continuity of scholastic teaching on labour and wages from the thirteenth to the eighteenth century.

envisaged as seeking the realization of an " ought-to-be " ; it is to this end that he has been given being and all created things have been placed at his disposal. God is to be glorified in every human act. Man is a free being, and therefore his actions, even the most trivial, are all significant; they either bring him nearer his goal or draw him away from it. Such a conception leaves no room for indifferent actions. In a world so conceived, there is no greater end than that of final beatitude, which is therefore the only ultimate end. And thus, if the spiritual progress of the individual is not to be impeded, there is no end but finds place in a hierarchical order, in which every end, however noble, is a middle term, and by this very fact cannot be attained by acts or means that are not at the same time acts or means for the attainment of the ultimate and supreme end. Man rises from earth to heaven by a stair at the head of which stands eternal beatitude. At certain distances there are intermediate stages to be reached in the ascent. Every step is a step nearer to the proximate stage, but also to the final one of all. If we try to reach the proximate stage obliquely, we lose the main stair and no longer progress towards the final goal.

This metaphor can give us an idea of the Catholic conception of life. A little reflection will show that there are no limits to the permeation of human activity by this conception. The moral necessity of attaining the ultimate end circumscribes human action in the domestic, the political, the economic, and the purely religious spheres. More exactly, we might say that such a conception transforms all activity into moral activity, and every act into a religious act. And thus man's ultimate end, whether he prays, works, studies, does business, eats, or amuses himself, is always God, and every means that leads him to study, work, do business, eat, and so forth, must at the same time be such as to lead him towards his attainment of the Beatific Vision. In other words, human action should be a continual prayer.[1]

God is the rationalizing term of human life; all human means will appear rational or irrational just in so far as they lead man towards the attainment of God.

In the various orders of acts that go to form the sum of human activity, rationalization of means will be determined by other ideas, but these can never conflict with the fundamental idea of all. Thus, for example, in the sphere of economic activity, the rationalizing idea will be that of the lowest possible cost, but it definitely cannot prevail beyond the point at which rationalization according to this principle ceases to mean rationalization according to God. Nor may we say that to begin with, within a given partial order, rationalization can be completed in accordance with the partial end, and the results subsequently rationalized in accordance with the ultimate end. Catholic ethics do not admit this successive rationalization, except in the case of a reparation for evil done. Catholic moral

---

[1] St. Paul, 1 *Cor.* x, 31.

doctrine demands that when the mediate end has determined a primary selection of means, these cannot be put into operation till further selection has been made in accordance with successively higher ends, the final choice being determined by the ultimate end of all. It is only then that lawful activity can begin.

If I, as a contractor, have to supply a factory with raw materials, I will try to obtain them at the lowest possible cost. But, as a Catholic, I must see whether in practice this economic criterion does not conflict with extra-economic ends higher than economic ends, for instance, social ends. If this conflict exists, I may not hesitate, and must choose the means that is economically more costly, but is, socially speaking, more rational. Then, supposing that the hierarchy of mediate ends is exhausted, I must see whether that means is rational from the standpoint of the attainment of God. If it is not so, I must still seek another; only when I have found this and adopted it, can my action lawfully begin.

By this example we believe we have completed our sketch of the general conception of economic life in Catholic moral teaching, and we can now proceed to consider its more definite implications in the economic sphere. We shall now deal with wealth, and the ways in which it may be acquired and used, so as to give a clear idea of the bonds laid by Catholicism on economic activity.

For Catholics, earthly goods are a means, and as means man not only may desire them, but he must take

123

possession of them for his corporal sustenance and for the relief of his neighbour.[1] Wealth, says Orlich,[2] becomes an evil when, instead of a means it becomes an end and absorbs human activity at the expense of the attainment of his eternal goal. For temporal goods " are subjected to man that he may use them according to his needs, not that he may place his end in them,"[3] " since riches are not man's highest good."[4]

From this idea spring all the rules as to the acquisition of goods. It has been said that these rules show a great mistrust of wealth,[5] but we should say rather that, in their awareness of the effects of the Fall, they reveal a great mistrust of men. " Argentum et aurum quod ad animi bonum spectat, nec bona sunt, nec mala : usus tamen horum bonus, abusio mala, sollicitudo pejor,

---

[1] St. Thomas, S.T., II–II, q. 83, art 6 : " Temporalia bona licet desiderare, . . . sicut quaedam adminicula, quibus adjuvamur ad tendendum in beatitudinem, inquantum scilicet per ea vita corporalis sustentatur et inquantum nobis organice deserviunt ad actus virtutum ; Contra gentes, I, 3, c. 134 : Exteriores divitiae sunt necessariae ad bonum virtutis, cum per eas sustentemus corpus et aliis subveniamus."

[2] A. Orlich, " L'uso dei beni nella morale di S. Tomaso " in La scuola cattolica, Milan, Years XL and XLI, October, 1912, p. 220.

[3] St. Thomas, S.T., II–II, q. 55, art. 6.

[4] St. Thomas, Contra gentes, I, 3, Chap. XXX.

[5] Cumusano (Saggi di economia politica e sc. delle finanze, Palermo, Tip. dello Statuto, 1887, pp. 39–42), Brants (op. cit., p. 30), and Marconcini (Le grandi linee della politica terriera e demografica di Roma da Gregorio I a Pio IX, Turin, Sit, 1931, pp. 67–9) protest against this opinion. Polier (L'idée du juste salaire, Paris, Giard, 1903, p. 27) believed himself justified in declaring that according to the Fathers of the Church, wealth is " l'ennemie de la vie morale."

It is certain that the Begards, heretics of the twelfth century, declared temporal goods to be useless and contemptible (Orlich, op. cit., October, 1912, p. 218), whereas St. Thomas considered them as necessary means. Such means were none too sympathetically viewed by the upholders of poverty (F. Tocco, La quistione della povertà nel sec. XIV, Naples, Perrella, 1910).

quoesus turpior."[1] Riches do not imply everlasting death ; circumspection and prudence may make rich men such as those to whom the Lord of the Saints gave counsel.[2] In 1304 Blessed Giordano da Rivalto preached as follows : " Misers are over head and ears in money and therefore they are drowned by it, but holy men put it under their feet and tread upon it and master it. . . . Of many Saints we read that they were very rich. They climbed up on this tower, on this mountain, and they were nearer to God. The more they had, and climbed up on it, the higher they were and the nearer to heaven, grateful to God for it and thanking him for it and loving him the more for it."[3] In this idea, that the evil lies not in possession of wealth but in making it the end of life, all the scholastics are agreed, from St. Thomas to St. Antonino of Florence, and Cardinal Gaetano.[4] Their teaching was reasserted in the Encyclicals of Leo XIII and Pius XI.[5]

Closely bound up with the idea of wealth as a means is the idea of private property, which, although all Catholics admit that natural law *determinavit in natura*

[1] St. Bernard, *De Consideratione*, I, II, Chap. VI, quoted by M. Vignes, *Les doctrines économiques, etc.*, op. cit., p. 555.

[2] St. Luke, VI.

[3] B. Giordano da Rivalto, *Prediche scelte*, Florence, Lib. Editr. Fiorentina, 1924, pp. 94–5.

[4] Cf. St. Antonino, *Opera omnia*, Venetiis, Poletti, MDCCXLV, vol. III, sermon V, art. I, p. 25 ; C. Ilgner, *Die volkswirtschaftlichen Anschauungen Antoninus von Florenz*, Paderborn, Schöningh, 1904, pp. 5–9 ; T. De Vio, Card. Caietanus ; *Opuscula oeconomico-socialia*, ed. P. Zammit, Romae, " Angelicum," 1934 ; A. Fanfani, *Le origini, etc.*, op. cit., pp. 106–7, and, in general, Chap. IV. for the other Scholastics of the fifteenth century.

[5] Leo XIII, *Rerum Novarum*, Pius XI, *Quadragesimo anno*.

umana hoc, quod omnia essent communia,[1] is not opposed
but accepted for various reasons.[2] The principle that
" all things are common " and the idea of wealth as a
means result in a conception of private property that is
much tempered and closely bound up with the rules as
to the social use of property. The interweaving of these
principles gives rise to corollaries determining the duties
of the rich man, who, in the words of Bourdaloue, is
such that he may relieve the poor, so much so that, for
Massillon, to the poor the rich man is Providence made
visible.[3]

This teaching, faithful to the spirit of the Gospels [4]
and of tradition,[5] has been restated as essentially Catholic
by recent Popes.[6] Conciliating opposing interests,
adhering to the principle of charity and neighbourly
love, it does not subvert the natural order, but perfects
it and integrates it in Christian civilization.

We believe we have now made the Catholic conception
of wealth and property sufficiently clear.

---

[1] Scoto, *Gent*, IV, 15, q. 2. Bossuet also said : " God from the beginning
of the world gave an equal right to all his creatures over all the things of which
they have need for the conservation of their life " (*Panégyrique de Saint
François d'Assise*).
[2] St. Thomas, *S.T.*, II–II, q. 66, art. 2. In this respect Leo XIII reiterated
Catholic principles against the Socialists (*Rerum Novarum*) and Pius XI
against the Catholic Socialists (*Quadragesimo anno*). On the doctrine of
Catholic Socialism, see B. Beham, *Religiöser Sozialismus*, Paderborn, Schöningh, 1933, especially Chaps. II and III.
[3] Bourdaloue, *Œuvres*, vol. I, p. 177 ; Massillon, *Petit Carême, Sermon de
l'Humanité des Grands envers le Peuple* (quoted by B. Groethuysen, op. cit.,
pp. 179–80).
[4] Mark x, 21 ; Luke iii, 11 ; xi, 41 ; xii, 33 ; xvi, 19–31 ; 2 Cor. viii,
13–14.
[5] Acts iv, 34 ; Tertullian, *Apology*, Chap. XXXIX.
[6] Leo XIII, *Rerum Novarum*, p. 23 ; Pius XI, *Quadragesimo anno*.

In an outlook on the world that makes God the centre, in a conception of life in which everything must facilitate the spiritual ascent of man to God, can Catholics admit any other idea of wealth ? To men in their banishment, nature offers an endless stair on which they may rise to God ; how can earthly goods fail to be steps in this stair ? Riches may be so considered if they are employed either as a means for corporal sustenance, in so far as the body is necessary to the operation of the soul, or else as a means for the corporal sustenance of those others who have not sufficient goods of their own.[1] Only economic action informed by these principles can be held lawful.

Wealth is thus a gift of God, and therefore not to be condemned. But men must not seek it so eagerly as to forget to lay up treasure in heaven, and they must walk carefully, for " the care of this world and the deceitfulness of riches choketh up the word." [2]

Such is the teaching of the New Testament ; such the teachings of the Fathers, the Doctors, the orthodox theologians of every age, who framed the rules that, sanctioned by the Popes, should order the economic activity of Catholics. Such has been the doctrine preached by the preachers of every age, whether they had the fresh humour of a St. Bernardino of Siena, or the prolix periods of a Segneri.[3]

[1] St. Thomas, *Contra gentes*, I, 3, Chap. CXXXIV : " Exteriores divitiae sunt necessariae ad bonum virtutis, cum per eas sustentemus et aliis subveniamus."

[2] Matthew vi, 19, and xiii, 22.

[3] P. Segneri, *Quaresimale*, XXII Sermon, p. 197 (in *Opera del Padre*

In respect of the acquisition of wealth, Catholic doctrine can be summarized as follows. Man has necessities, needs that must be satisfied, and, if temporal goods can satisfy them, it is a duty and legitimate to seek to acquire such goods, bearing in mind two rules, first that they must be acquired by lawful means, secondly that the amount acquired must not exceed the need. These two rules restrict respectively the choice and the use of means of procuring wealth. A failure to respect such limits would be an offence against God, an infraction of the rules of justice, honesty, and moderation; a subversion of the divine order, which has provided goods to supply the needs of all, and not for the greed of a few; with the risk that man, in his anxiety for goods, might forget the Creator. On this point, St. Thomas expresses himself thus: the desire of wealth is unlawful if we seek it as an ultimate end, if we seek it with too great solicitude, or if we fear that, by following conscience, we shall lack necessities. In other words, solicitude about temporal things may be unlawful in three ways: " first on the part of the object of solicitude,

Segneri, vol. II, Venice, 1773): " Therefore, O rich men, O men concerned with your own interests, O insatiable ones, where are you? Why do you journey as exiles from your fathers' homes to gather together more money? Why do you cross so many Appennines? Why do you pass over so many Alps? Why do you lose yourselves in so many seas? . . . Turn back your prows to the land, and do not seek to trust your lives to fragile ships. Do you seek anything more than to fill your granaries? Than to fill your cellars to overflowing? Here is the way. Every day by your alms do honour to God. . . ." Earlier, in the same sermon, Segneri has pointed out (p. 193) that the rich are masters indeed, but not absolute masters, since they have " the obligation . . . to share among the poor what remains after honest provision for their own estate."

that is, if we seek temporal things as an end. . . .
Secondly . . . through too much earnestness in
endeavouring to obtain temporal things, the result being
that a man is drawn away from spiritual things which
ought to be the chief object of his search. . . . Thirdly,
through overmuch fear, when, to wit, a man fears to
lack necessary things if he does what he ought to do." [1]

Outside these cases, that is to say, when a man in
seeking temporal goods does so to supply his needs, the
endeavour to obtain riches is not unlawful, but praise-
worthy, the solicitude of a man who gains his bread by
bodily labour is not superfluous, but proportionate. [2]
Thus work and the acquisitive effort are justifiable
and to be encouraged ; though in general they are only
considered legitimate up to the point of the satisfaction
of the necessities involved. [3] For, on the contrary, the
efforts of a man who after satisfying his needs continues
to work so as to gain fresh wealth, either in order to
reach a higher social position, or to make his sons
richer and more powerful than himself, are—in the words
of Henry of Langenstein [4]—signs of avarice, sensuality,
or pride, and therefore necessarily to be condemned. [5]

---

[1] St. Thomas, *S.T.*, II–II, q. 55, art. 6.
[2] St. Thomas, *S.T.*, II–II, q. 55, art. 6.
[3] Tawney (op. cit., p. 35) writes : " The mediæval theorist condemned
as a sin precisely that effort to achieve a continuous and unlimited increase
in material wealth which modern societies applaud as a quality."
[4] E. di Langenstein, *Tractatus bipartitus de contractibus emptionis et vendi-
tionibus*, I, 13, quoted by E. Schreiber, *Die volkswirtschaftlichen Anschauungen
der Scholastik seit Thomas von Aquin*, Jena, Fischer, 1913, p. 197.
[5] The French preachers of the eighteenth century continue to condemn it
(B. Groethuysen, op. cit., pp. 229–30). The Italian Segneri only allows a
man to improve his position without altering his social rank, and mistrusts

It might be objected that Pius XI modified these principles when he wrote: "those who are engaged in production are not forbidden to increase their fortunes in a lawful and just manner; indeed it is right that he who renders service to society and enriches it, should himself have his proportionate share of the increased social wealth . . . ," but it will soon be seen that he conforms to the spirit of the principles we have set forth. For he goes on to say that such increased wealth is lawful " provided always that in seeking this he respects the laws of God and the rights of others, and uses his property in accord with faith and right reason." The Pope's teaching on this point [1] tends less towards the formal letter of Thomism than towards its interpretation in St. Bernardino of Siena, who prefers a man to enrich himself in order to profit his neighbour by new enterprizes, rather than to sit idle for fear of growing too rich.[2]

It might indeed be thought that even if the principles we have set forth were accepted, a bolder and constant effort to work for gain would be justifiable from the point of view of future needs. Here is a big question, for the Gospel precept "take no thought for

" a peasant who seeks to become a citizen, a citizen who seeks to become a knight . . . a knight who seeks to become the son of a ruler " (P. Segneri, " Quaresimale " in *Opere*, Sermon XX, vol. II, p. 196).

[1] Pius XI, *Quadragesimo Anno*.

[2] St. Bernardino, *Prediche volgari dette sulla piazza del Campo l'anno MCCCCXXVII*, ed. Bianchi, Siena, 1880, vol. III, p. 204, and *Opera omnia*, vol. I, Sermon XLVI, art. III, Chap. IV. St. Bernardino's theories have been treated in Chap. IV of our own work on the origins of the capitalistic spirit, also by M. Sticco, in his excellent little book, *Il pensiero sociale di San Bernardino* (Milan, S. E., " Vita e Pensiero," 1925).

to-morrow " [1] seems at first sight to forbid any concern for future needs, and might be taken as condemning any endeavour to provide for to-morrow as well as for to-day. Nor could appeal be made to the virtue of prudence, for St. Thomas declares that " prudence regards things which are directed to the end of life as a whole," whereas " prudence of the flesh," for which the ultimate end lies in worldly things, " is a sin." [2]

On the other hand, side by side with the " take no thought " of the Gospel, we find a passage in *Proverbs*, one of the inspired books, which counsels us to learn from the ant, which " although she hath no guide, nor master, nor captain, Provideth her meat for herself in the summer, and gathereth her food in the harvest." [3] The Angelic Doctor brings this exhortation and the Gospel prohibition into harmony by pointing out that the Lord, with His " take no thought," sought to forbid any thought for the morrow beyond its needs, while the spirit of the Gospels can be accurately interpreted as follows : man must concern himself with the future only at the right time and within just limits.[4] The foresight of the ant, on the other hand, is praised " because the ant is solicitous at a befitting time, and it is this that is proposed for our example." [5] Therefore, a man may work with a view to gain, not only to provide for the needs of to-day, but also for those future, more than

[1] Matthew vi, 34.
[2] St. Thomas, *S.T.*, II–II, q. 55, art. 1.
[3] *Proverbs* vi, 6.
[4] St. Thomas, *S.T.*, II–II, q. 55, art. 7.
[5] St. Thomas, *S.T.*, II–II, q. 55, art. 7.

probable, needs, for which he does not expect to be able to provide when they are upon him. Foresight, says St. Thomas, must be reasonable. In short, it is necessary to be careful lest excessive anxiety for gain, driven out by the door, should come back by the window. Thus, to work and gain is legitimate so long as work and gain seek the satisfaction of *praesentis vitae necessitatem*, and the anticipation of future needs does not mask an accumulation in excess of need. Nor is excess of work justified by Thomism if it is directed to a betterment of social position, since everyone should be content with the state in life in which he finds himself, and seek to keep up the position he has, no more. None the less, the rigidity of Thomism has been tempered by Gaetano's interpretation, by which a man endowed with exceptional qualities may lawfully seek the wealth that will procure him a status compatible with his qualities.[1]

The question now rises, is it lawful to save ? To this we shall reply later. For the moment, let us see by what means gain can honestly be sought within the prescribed limits.

The chief means by which a man can gain a sufficiency for his needs is work. If the word is taken in its widest sense, there are indeed no others, unless we include such exceptional and uncertain means as treasure-trove or legacies.

---

[1] T. De Vio, Cardinal Gaetano, *Comm. in Summa Theol. Thom.*, II–II, q. 118, art. 1.

No classes of work are to be preferred above the rest, so long as the worker respects the principles we have set forth, and St. Paul's exhortation: *that no man overreach nor circumvent his brother in business.*[1]

The principles on which mediæval Catholicism based its antipathy towards commerce[2] have been in part maintained, in part abandoned. A more accurate idea of production has dissipated suspicion of the trader, who is no longer considered a parasite.[3] But the Scholastic mistrust of the perils encountered by the trader is shared by modern writers[4] and has not wholly vanished even to-day. This reserve, inasmuch as it reveals a fear lest the purity of manners be threatened by commercial relations, shows the unchanging determination of Catholicism to renounce the benefits of natural works rather than obstruct the work of salvation. The fulfilment of the work of salvation should be man's basic concern, and it is not dearly bought by the renunciation of some human advantage which is not despised but reputed of less account than eternal happiness. The mediæval prejudices against commerce, which were founded on its reputed unproductiveness, have vanished. But with the persistence of the Christian conception of

---

[1] St. Paul, 1 *Thess.* iv, 6.

[2] A. Fanfani, *Le origini, etc.,* p. 10.

[3] Such was the common opinion in the tenth century (P. Boissonnade, *Life and Work in Mediæval Europe,* Eng. tr., London and New York, 1927, p. 159).

[4] Thomassin, *Traité du negoce et de l'usure,* 1697; De la Gibonais, *De l'usure, intérêt et profit qu'on tire du prêt . . . ,* 1710, quoted by Groethuysen; P. Segneri, " Il Cristiano istruito " in *Opera,* vol. III, Part I, Section XXVI, art. 6.

133

life the rules remain that made of commerce a means of acquiring wealth, and a significant means to the ends involved in the attainment of the sole eternal good.

It is this conviction that leads Catholic writers to speak of a just price in transactions,[1] and to insist that traders must not sell one thing for another, or adulterate their goods, or give false measure, or procure unlawful gain by working on holidays of obligation. These ordinances are valid for all who have occasion to exchange goods or services ; the same principles hold good for the employers in respect of conditions and remuneration of labour. In this case, the just price will be a just wage, but the principle involved is still one of commutative justice, and the higher control of morality over the remotest spheres of economic life is reasserted.

Taking its stand on a moral principle, Catholic doctrine confronts another economic problem of great importance, that of interest. On this subject Catholic writers, basing themselves on the well-known phrase in the Gospels, which they later reinforced by considerations on the unfruitfulness of money, taken over from Greek philosophy, have maintained from earliest times[2] that to lend at interest is *per se* unlawful, whereas causes extraneous to the loan itself may justify the lender in asking for compensation. This doctrine has persisted

---

[1] On the Scholastic and mediæval theory of the just price, see the studies by Cairoli, Hagenauer, Arias, quoted on pp. 12–3 of *Le origini, etc.* (Fanfani). In the same book there is a concise account of the theory, on which, recently, Sapori has also written (*Il giusto prezzo nella dottrina di S. Tomaso e nella pratica del tempo*, art. quoted).

[2] A. Fanfani, *Le origini, etc.*, p. 15.

unchanged, though it has been lately made more precise by recognition that there are a greater number of such extraneous causes than was realized by moralists up to the eighteenth century.[1] Anxiety to ensure the respect of morality in this sphere so predominated that for a long time moralists encouraged men to meet the necessities of economic life, not by the simple means of a loan, but by association in companies. Thus a solution that was rational both morally and economically, such as that of association, was given precedence over a solution that was rational only economically. This is a plain example of how the Catholic spirit subordinates economic to moral problems.

We could dwell at length on this question, but the result would be a casuistry useless to the scholar and bewildering to the reader facing such problems for the first time. The informing principles that give an unmistakable Catholic imprint to economic life and activity remain firm; we shall soon see how such an imprint can hardly harmonize with capitalistic practice.

If the principles we have mentioned are valid for the acquisition of wealth, there are others that hold good

---

[1] Père Hyacinthe de Gasquet (*L'usure démasquée*, 1776, p. 62) not only declares against the remuneration of a loan, but maintains that his opinion was reinforced by a similar outlook among the doctors of the Sorbonne of his time (Groethuysen, op. cit., p. 251). For Father Segneri's rigid views on the question, see his work: " Il Cristiano istruito " in *Opera*, vol. III, part I, section XVIII, art. VI, p. 165. The year before the death of this famous preacher, M. Bonaventura Padovano printed a pamphlet (*L'usura convinta con la ragione*, Ferrara-Treviso, Curti, 1693) in which he not only sought to prove that usury was " forbidden by the laws, Natural, Divine and Evangelical " (pp. 23 and 151), but aimed at suggesting the means which, though less profitable, were more pleasing to God, and which could take its place (p. 160).

for its use. Man may use it moderately and temperately. He must use it to provide for his present and anticipated needs and for the needs of those dependent on him. Surplus wealth must be used to provide also for the needs of his neighbour.[1]

The fact that surplus must be devoted to the needs of the poor seems to rule out any principle of provision for the future and to condemn all saving. On this point Catholic doctrine has established a distinction. To work simply in order to save is unlawful. But for a man to work to provide for anticipated future needs, to expand his business so as to better his own position and profit his neighbour and his country, is most lawful, and this according to both old and modern formulations of Catholic thought, according to the Angelic Doctor and according to the reigning Pope.[2]

In substance, even in the matter of savings, the principles of equilibrium, the just mean, the social use of goods, and the subordination of corporal to spiritual advantage, demand a moderation that is incompatible with either the miser's meanness or the spendthrift's generosity, just as it is incompatible with the anxieties of a man who sees in each economic action solely an operation productive of wealth.

[1] For this problem, and in general for all problems inherent in the use of wealth, see the Scholastic solutions in Fanfani, *Le origini*, op. cit., Chaps. I and IV. It also contains a bibliography of ancient and recent works. For recent doctrine on the question, cf. *Rerum Novarum* and *Quadragesimo Anno*.

[2] St. Thomas, *S.T.*, II–II, q. 78, art. 4; Pius XI, *Quadragesimo Anno*. On the mediæval theologians, cf. A. Fanfani, *Le origini*, etc., pp. 22–3, 116–7, 125–6.

2. The capitalistic conception of life is founded on a separation of human aims. It fixes its gaze on natural and in particular on economic goals; it precludes supernatural, religious goals.[1] It does not deny that a religious order may exist either in reality or in human belief, but it does not conceive of this order as able to conflict with the economic order; still less that it could contain the economic order so as to bring its laws into harmony with its own. In the capitalistic organization of life priority is given to a criterion of rationalization, a principle of order, that is, of economic nature. Its innovation lay in the adoption of this criterion as the autonomous principle of what it envisaged as an equally autonomous order. If the existence of other proximate or higher orders is admitted, they remain distinct; it is as such that they are to be brought into harmony one with another, and with the whole of which they are component parts. In themselves they remain impermeable to extraneous influences; the intervention of other principles of order brings disorder. In the purely capitalistic outlook there is only one principle of rationalization—failing the admission of others, as an extreme concession of which man will bear the full consequences, which, as they come into play, make complete rationalization in accordance with the main criterion impossible, and prevent the attainment of those maximum results that a single principle of rationalization could provide.

Capitalism has one principle: individual economic

[1] B. Groethuysen, op. cit., pp. viii and 51.

utility. The choice of means and actions must be determined by their aptness to this end. The principle of individual economic utility as ultimate end and principle of order is the criterion by which means and actions are chosen. It regulates, too, the organization of such means, and tends to create a general atmosphere in which such activities will have the fullest scope.

When these ideals are put into practice, the result, as we saw in the last chapter, is a society so organized as to leave the maximum autonomy to the individual, who in most cases is forced to adopt the utility criterion as his norm of action, in order not to expose himself to loss.

Given the aspirations and ends of capitalism, the natural organization of social life in a capitalistic age is that of political and economic liberalism, and precisely in such an environment the law of risk automatically regulates the development of capitalism. Once this way has been opened, many will feel it inevitable to go forward, others will deem it more profitable, and others will feel it impossible to arrest their course or turn back. Once the social organization has adopted the aims of capitalism, it adopts its standards of judgment, hence its ideas of just and unjust, fitting and unfitting, normal and abnormal. In consequence, it forges those instruments that by such standards seem efficient for the attainments of such aims.

To discover a principle on which to base criticism of a system like that of capitalism within that system is impossible. Criticism can only come from another order of ideas, from a system that would direct social activity towards non-capitalistic ends. This Catholicism does when its social ethics demand that ends must converge in a definitely non-capitalistic direction. Not that Catholicism rejects economic rationalization, or that it wishes this to be brought about by principles foreign to the economic order, but it holds that such rationalization should be bounded by the other principles that order life.[1]

With its principles, Catholicism, which is definitely voluntarist, cannot consent to leave human activity to the pressure of events. Still less can it give the palm to that social organization in which a predominant interest receives the full sanction of the law, regardless of its positive or negative relations with the aim of society, of the State, of man, as Catholicism understands it. Catholic ethics, in virtue of the ends they set before man and society and of the Catholic conception of human nature and creation, is necessarily in favour of State intervention, and cannot, for instance, approve when the State concedes full and unlimited " freedom

[1] Pius XI, *Quadragesimo Anno*, p. 52 : " All those versed in social matters earnestly demand a rational reorganization in order to bring back economic life to sound and true order. But this order, which We Ourselves most earnestly desire and make every effort to promote, will be quite faulty and imperfect, unless all man's activities harmoniously unite to imitate and, as far as it is humanly possible, attain the marvellous unity of the Divine plan. This is the perfect order which the Church preaches with intense earnestness, and which right reason demands ; which places God as the first and supreme end of all created activity, and regards all created goods as mere instruments under God, to be used only in so far as they help towards the attainment of our supreme end."

of labour," [1] wholly regardless of consequences to the worker and society—even if this neglect could be justified by the conviction—denied by Catholic philosophy, that the conciliation of interests comes about automatically. Whereas such an attitude on the part of the State is one of the postulates of capitalism where it has not reached the development of Communism.

Here we are not discussing which of the two conceptions—of which the facts noted are corollaries—is right, or which is profitable. We are observing and comparing them, showing their fundamental contradiction. This plain opposition throws considerable doubt, to say the least, on the assertion that Catholicism, as a body of doctrine, has favoured the capitalistic outlook, and hence the advent of capitalism.

In an age in which the Catholic conception of life had a real hold over the mind, capitalistic action could only have manifested itself as something erroneous, reprehensible, spasmodic, and sinful, to be condemned by the faith and knowledge of the agent himself. Never could such an age have seen the beginning of the century-long development that has brought capitalistic society into being. Such an age would not have been ignorant of machinery and technical progress, for the Church would have had neither wish nor means to intervene

---

[1] *Codice sociale, Schema di una sintesi sociale cattolica*, art. 70 : "Freedom of labour, in its historical signification, means a state of affairs in which, under pretext of respecting the individual freedom of the worker, all organization of labour by means of the trade or the State is ruled out. Such a condition of affairs is in contradiction to Catholic doctrine as expounded by Leo XIII in his Encyclical *Rerum Novarum*."

to judge or impede them.[1] But assuredly, every time machinery and technical progress brought the smallest pressure to bear on the moral and social sphere,[2] Catholic ethics would have put a check on them.[3] As a matter of fact, we cannot doubt that in a perfectly Catholic age purely technical progress would not have found such powerful incentives as in a capitalistic civilization. Economic life shows itself more active, with greater quantitative results, where the economic end is uncontested. Where this end is circumscribed by the endeavour to attain simultaneously to other ends, it is obvious that the development of the economic means is sacrificed. As a result economic life will manifest itself in forms not only qualitatively different, but producing smaller quantitative results.

But if the Catholic Church often finds nothing to which to take exception in the private instruments of capitalism,[4] she finds much to blame in the end to which they are directed and the manner in which they are organized. Still more does she deplore that the life of the capitalistically minded man falls outside her orbit. The Catholic moralist cannot fail to disapprove of such

[1] Pius XI, *Quadr. agesimo anno.*

[2] Toniolo (*Trattato di economia sociale, Introduzione,* 3rd ed., Florence, Libr. Editr. Fiorentina, pp. 301–2) has some very fine reflections on this subject.

[3] The *Codice Sociale,* for instance, writes as follows (art. 72) : "However commendable in certain respects are the methods known as 'Taylorism,' which seek by various means, and especially by the introduction of methodical rhythm, to increase the yield of labour, we must none the less be on the watch for any deviation that would turn the worker into an automaton and practically deprive him of the exercise of his human faculties."

[4] F. Vito, "La 'Q. a.' e i problemi dell' economia moderna " in *Rivista Internazionale di Scienze Sociali,* 1931, pp. 335–6.

a life when he notes how " The day is not long enough for the overwhelming occupations of the capitalists; they deny themselves the rest of which even slaves are not deprived; night rivals day in respect of their assiduous labour; meals, rest, everything is broken by business—payments, commissions, accounts; everything conspires to hold them in anxiety and bondage, which barely leave them the freedom to remember that they are Christians."[1]

Moreover, the Catholic conception cannot grant the individualism that is a postulate of capitalism, still less can it agree that society should be organized on an individualistic basis. This is why the Popes of the last two centuries have so definitely condemned liberalism, seeking to circumscribe its effects in the economic and social spheres by indirect and direct encouragement of social legislation, and looking forward to the time when it should give place to a corporative organization of society.[2]

Catholicism cannot recognize certain liberties in the absence of which capitalism becomes transformed and dies. Capitalism requires such a dread of loss, such a forgetfulness of human brotherhood, such a certainty that a man's neighbour is merely a customer to be gained or a rival to be overthrown, and all these are inconceivable in the Catholic conception of the world. In other

---

[1] P. Croiset, *Réflexions chrétiennes sur divers sujets de morale*, ed. 1752, vol. II, p. 261, quoted by Groethuysen (op. cit., p. 240).

[2] See " Chronological repertory of pontifical documents on social problems " in appendix to *Le encicliche sociali di Leone XIII e Pio XI*, Milan, " Vita e Pensiero," 1933.

words, Catholic concern for the subsistence of the whole cannot be reconciled with capitalistic concern to find the best formula for production in respect of a single undertaking. The latter marks the triumph of technique, the former should mark the mastery of man over formulas.

But at bottom the true and deep-seated reason for the conflict between Catholic and capitalistic ethics, lies—let us repeat—in the diverse manner of correlating human actions in general and economic actions in particular to God. The Catholic, as we have said, appraises the legality of every action by the criteria of Revelation. The capitalist does not doubt the lawfulness of any act that fully corresponds to what he considers the exigences of human reason. The Catholic order is a supernatural order, the capitalistic order is a rational order in the sense of the Enlightenment.

We might continue with examples and comparisons, but we should find nothing to make us modify our conclusion that there is an unbridgeable gulf between the Catholic and the capitalistic conception of life.

If European history knew a pre-capitalistic age, it is in that age that we must seek for a trend of public life and private activity in harmony with the social principles of Catholicism. This we think we have proved in an earlier publication; we recall it here as ground for declaring that when Catholic ethics have been a prevailing influence in public life, the result has been for various institutions and laws to co-ordinate the activity of private individuals in non-capitalistic orders.

This does not mean that the predominance of Catholic ideals in mediæval society was responsible for all the characteristics of mediæval economy. It means instead that these ideals directed the economic system, which was the outcome of various historical factors, towards definitely non-capitalistic aims. If we consider the system against its background, we shall not fail to recognize the positive influence of Catholicism. If we consider the means it employed, we note their relation to other historical contingencies through which the life of the age took its course.

With the passage of time, for reasons that we shall examine in the next chapter, instruments are perfected and transformed, and men aspire to another organization of society. Catholicism, as long as it exerts an influence on public life, seeks to hinder those innovations that are opposed to the realization of such a system as it envisages. Through the Sacrament of Penance and preaching, an attempt is made to arrest the trend towards autonomy of morals; insatiable anxiety over business is condemned, and individualistic achievements implying only personal advantage are deprecated. The anti-capitalistic action of the Church, which was very intense in the fifteenth and sixteenth centuries,[1] was still, as

---

[1] A. Fanfani, *Le origini*, etc., op. cit., Chap. IV. In respect of the sixteenth century, we have made use of the early results of the research of G. Barbieri, who is engaged in a work on the subject that we were able to see privately. Gobbi (*L'economia politica negli scrittori italiani del secolo XVI-XVII*, Milan, Hoepli, 1889, pp. 338–9 and 351–62) has shown who and how many among Italian writers during this period remained faithful to Catholic teaching on wealth, interest, etc.

Groethuysen has pointed out, in full force in the eighteenth century,[1] but none the less it cannot be said to have been successful. It is true that the Church exerted a positive influence, so much so that in the eighteenth century the anonymous author of *La Théorie de l'Intérêt de l'Argent* (p. 184) bears witness that " among the capitalists of the kingdom probably about a third do not dare traffic with their capital and direct it into the channels of trade, some for fear of being branded as usurers, others in order not to wound or burden their conscience." [2]

In spite of this, the forces of capitalism end by triumphing, and the new ideas transform society. From this moment—between the end of the eighteenth century and the beginning of the nineteenth—the influence of Catholic ethics greatly diminishes, but this does not mean approval of the new situation. It might be said, on the contrary, that the Church has done her utmost to discriminate between those novelties that were the healthy product of the age and those that derived from the human mind emancipated from religious check.

After a period of stasis, the struggle begins again ; this time it is entrusted to a minority of scholars and men of action, to whom the task is assigned of demanding the reform of society.[3] Criticism and protests from the

---

[1] B. Groethuysen, op. cit., passim.
[2] B. Groethuysen, op. cit., p. 272.
[3] M. Zanatta, *I tempi e gli uomini che prepararono la " Rerum Novarum,"* Milan, Soc. Ed. " Vita e Pensiero," 1931 ; G. Dalla Torre, " Le aspirazioni corporative dei cattolici e i documenti pontifici " in the May number of *Vita e Pensiero,* 1934.

clergy, studies, programmes of action and organizations on the part of the laity, reinforce the attacks of the growing number of those dissatisfied with the capitalist system. Catholics, side by side with workers' and reformist groups, demand social legislation. This is the plainest testimony to the anti-capitalistic attitude[1] of the Catholic forces concerned. It meant non-recognition of the autonomy of the economic subject, a negation of the domination of the law of risk, a restatement of the social duties implied by property, a recognition that the State has a faculty of intervention over and above the concessions of citizens. It signifies, moreover, a declaration that the truth of the liberal and capitalistic doctrine is not to be recognized; that harmony of interests can only spring from an exchange of positive collaboration, in which not only the man with capital, but even the man who has nothing but his own personality to defend, is called upon to play his part. That the total well-being of the community does not spring from the activity of the employer, unless the community as a whole enjoys a healthy and prosperous life and is adequately protected from the play of purely economic interests. That dread of economic loss is not a sufficient reason to prevent the realization of higher interests. Catholic thought reveals itself most non-

---

[1] Heimann (*Soziale Theorie des Kapitalismus*, Tübingen, Mohr, 1929) notes the anti-capitalistic character of social policy. For other and diverse opinions, see A. Uggè, *La legislazione e l'organizzazione del lavoro* in " Atti della XII settimana sociale dei cattolici italiani," Milan, Soc. Ed., *Vita e Pensiero*, 1925, pp. 194-5.

capitalistic when, justified by such thought,[1] those who accept it demand the transformation of the social system in such a way that the provisional conquests achieved by social legislation shall become final and more vast through the establishment of the Corporation.[2]

It is in vain that certain writers seek to prove a decline in the positive influence of the Catholic religion on the developments of capitalism by the hypothesis that certain moralists sought to strip their doctrine of those maxims that might seem hostile to the nascent bourgeoisie.[3] This hypothesis has a certain value, inasmuch as it is based on the observation, substantially true, that at different periods preachers in particular sought to present Catholic doctrine under the aspects that would

[1] Full justification came with the promulgation of *Rerum Novarum* by Leo XIII, and which was elaborated by the *Quadragesimo Anno* of Pius XI. Basing itself on the teaching of *Rerum Novarum*, the International Union of Social Studies drew up a scheme of Catholic social synthesis under the title of *Codice Sociale* (It. ed. Rovigo, Ist. Ven. d'Arti Grafici, 1927).

[2] On the action of Catholics after *Rerum Novarum*, and on the influence of such action on social policy, see E. Martin Saint-Leon, *L'Encyclique " Rerum Novarum " et l'organisation professionelle en France* ; O. Schilling, *Die deutsche Sozialpolitik und die Enzyklika " Rerum novarum "* ; H. Somerville, *The Catholic Social Movement in England* ; M. Turmann, *Léon XIII, les catholiques sociaux et les origines de la législation internationale du travail* ; A. Valensin, *L'Encyclique " Rerum novarum " et les clauses ouvrières du Pacte de la Société des Nations* ; F. Vito, *Lo sviluppo dalla politica sociale in Germania e le direttive della " Rerum novarum "* ; L. Watt, " *Rerum novarum* " *and the Evolution of Capitalism in Great Britain*. All these are contained in the volume *Il XL anniversario della enciclica " Rerum novarum,"* Milan, " Vita e Pensiero," 1931. See also M. Turmann, *Le développement du catholicisme social depuis l'encyclique " Rerum novarum,"* Paris, 1900 ; P. Jostok, *Der deutsche Katholizismus und die Ueberwindung des Kapitalismus,* Regensburg, Pustet, 1932 ; P. Moon, *The Labor Problem and the Social Movement in France,* New York, Macmillan, 1921, Chaps. VI and VII.

[3] The hypothesis was put forward by Groethuysen (op. cit., pp. 54 et sq.) and repeated by Robertson (op. cit., p. 165), in whose work we find many echoes of Groethuysen. To confute it, J. Brodrick wrote *The Economic Morals of the Jesuits,* London, H. Milford, 1934.

least offend their hearers—thus imitating St. Paul among the Athenians. But the hypothesis falls to the ground if it is made to imply definite omissions in doctrinal teaching in order to please certain groups of the faithful. Certainly, new problems led to new formulations, which may have appeared more favourable to capitalistic groups than did the naked principle,[1] but this does not mean any mutilation of doctrine. In respect of this pretended adaptation of Catholic social ethics, there is a point of which we have found no mention : that a precept has different force in different contingencies ; it is therefore natural that in a capitalistic world the pressure of competition would decrease the necessity for a Catholic to resist certain particular phenomena that prevent him from observing a given moral law. It is in a way the question of the state of necessity which, in cases of grave and unjust injury, may justify a Catholic in conduct that apparently does not conform to the strict principle of morals involved.[2] But an observer of these facts, instead of deducing from them a weakening in Catholic moral teaching, should reflect that the facts themselves find their justification in principles that have always been proper to the morals of Catholicism.

Nevertheless, it cannot be wholly denied that the

---

[1] For instance, the successive elucidations in respect of the lawfulness of compensation (albeit determined by extrinsic causes) on occasion of loans.

[2] Cf. what we said on this matter in a note, " Caratteri delle regole in materia economica dettate dagli scolastici medioevali " in *Rivista di filosofia neoscolastica*, May-June, 1932.

intervention of Catholic precepts in favour of this or that institution (private property, respect of personality, limitation of absolutism, etc.) may have encouraged similar affirmations on the part of capitalism. But such action cannot be interpreted as encouragement of capitalism, just as no one maintains that it encouraged the invention of the motor car, or iron foundries. The essence of capitalism, which does not consist in this or that aspect of it (nearly all such aspects being accidental), can only meet with the most decided repugnance on the part of Catholicism.

Sombart has said that none the less Catholic ethics have contributed to the formation of the bourgeois mentality, if not by directing it at its source, at least by encouraging some of its particular expressions. Thus, for example, Catholicism has favoured such a bourgeois virtue as hard work.[1]

This assertion is based on a misunderstanding. We may answer, adopting Groethuysen's argument,[2] that for the Christian hard work is a means of penance ; for the bourgeois a means to success. Moreover, the hard work praised by Catholic moralists has a different inspiration from that of the bourgeois ; only in seeming are the two the same. That of the Catholic is a sign of homage to God, that of the bourgeois the expression of a lack of trust in Providence. The bourgeois, as we may read in the typical dialogues of Leon Battista Alberti,[3]

[1] W. Sombart, *Der Bourgeois*, op. cit., p. 310.
[2] B. Groethuysen, op. cit., pp. 215–6, 257–8.
[3] L. B. Alberti, *I primi tre libri della famiglia*, passim.

seeks by hard work to anticipate the most unthinkable future needs; it is an instrument in the service of individual thrift, a defence against possible and terrifying poverty. Bourgeois presumption is the opposite of the trusting indifference of the Christian[1]; the industry of both, though expressing itself in the same forms, has a different meaning, a different origin, a different end. Kraus has correctly interpreted the Catholic moralists when he says that their encouragement of industry in the fifteenth century does not aim at giving an impetus to a tendency to capitalistic gain, but was conceded in support of the just price theory and in rejection of the idea of living on income without working.[2]

We may add that intense industry, even that which exceeds individual needs, is socially justifiable for the Catholic philosopher, who, following in the steps of St. Bernardino, will point out that even the man who has gained sufficient for his own needs should seek to increase the prosperity of the whole community. Sombart, overlooking such considerations, has further pointed out that Catholic moralists in the Middle Ages taught what would be definitely a bourgeois virtue— honesty.[3] We make the same answer as before. The man who respects Catholic teaching is honest in order that he shall not offend God, the bourgeois is honest

[1] Lapo Mazzei, a typically pre-capitalist Catholic, writes in his *Letters* (op. cit., vol. I, p. 173): " When I die, these children will have to ask for bread. . . . But God first, of Whom the Gospel says that He has care for the sparrow, let alone the nourishment of men."

[2] J. Kraus, op. cit., p. 63.

[3] W. Sombart, *Der Bourgeois*, op. cit., p. 311.

(and here we adopt the arguments of Alberti, the first bourgeois, as Sombart himself confesses) in order to gain a good reputation, to be trusted, to gain preference in business transactions, to prosper. At the origin of bourgeois virtue we find eagerness for gain, which the moralists attack at every turn.

Again, the German sociologist remarks that Catholic ethics, by condemning prodigality and avarice and praising liberality, lay the foundations of the bourgeois mean in the administration of goods.[1] We must point out that in that case the whole of Christian morals, by which man is considered as the administrator of goods for which he must render account to God, encourages the advent of the bourgeois mind. But this cannot be said, in the same way that, as Groethuysen confesses,[2] it cannot be said that it was the Church that taught the bourgeois the virtue of order, as a means of golden mediocrity, for the bourgeois could not accept such teaching, set as he was upon " organizing his life outside the sphere of Providence." Once for all, to avoid useless discussion, we say that the spirit of the two conceptions is utterly different, and, as Brey has written, Christian and capitalistic virtues correspond in name but not in signification.[3]

In their general lines, Catholic social ethics are always antithetical to those of capitalism. It may none the less come about that here and there a less rigorous inter-

[1] W. Sombart, *Der Bourgeois*, op. cit., p. 310.
[2] B. Groethuysen, op. cit., pp. 198–212 and 220–1.
[3] H. Brey, op. cit., pp. 47–55.

pretation of this or that point may have favoured a mental trend towards capitalism. Thus to some it may seem not altogether too daring to say that the late Scholastic doctrine on tyrannicide gave a certain encouragement to individualistic aspirations, both political and economic, precisely in an age when the yoke of princes lay heaviest on their subjects. But considerations of this kind are out of place, since, after all, it is easy to prove that, inasmuch as they sprang from a particular interpretation of Catholic doctrine, they concern effects that should be attributed not to the doctrine, but to the men who so variously interpreted it. Thus if the tyrannicide theories really encouraged capitalistic individualism, this supposed effect should be attributed to the action of certain Catholics, not to Catholic doctrine. As times change, the force of such interpretations varies between a maximum and minimum ; now they may assist the development of capitalism, and now impede it, so that their results tend to cancel out, and, as a rule, may be left out of count [1] unless more accurate and detailed investigations prove them to have had a greater importance than now appears. Such investigations would be confined to the effects— whether great or small, we cannot tell—produced by a single fact, in a single country, and within the space of a

[1] With what is plainly exaggeration, Robertson (op. cit., p. 107) maintains that the probabilism of certain Catholic currents opened the way to the triumphs of capitalistic ethics. Brodrick, in the work we have already mentioned, calls the attention of scholars to the shaky foundations of Robertson's thesis.

few years. The very fact that such effects are eventually the result of an interpretation of principles makes it impossible for them to have any wide range or to be long-lasting, since their cause is not universally present wherever there are Catholics ; nor can it operate uncontested, for a doctrine can have many interpretations, even if all are orthodox. All capitalistic symptoms, manifested not by Catholic doctrine, but by the action of individual Catholics, whether Popes, Doctors, or the faithful, and whether few or many, will be limited in the same manner. In order to gain an idea of these partial effects, we will conclude our chapter with the following indications.

3. Our outline of Catholic social ethics will have made it clear that Catholics, so long as they held closely to the social teachings of the Church, could never act in favour of capitalism. Certainly no one can deny that such men as the Bardi, Pitti, Datini, acted in a capitalistic manner, and, though baptized Christians, introduced a capitalistic mode of life among their Catholic contemporaries. But we deny that in so doing they were acting in conformity with Catholic social ethics. Although they were baptized, we cannot take their action as a ground for judging the action of Catholics and the progress of capitalism. Otherwise, our task would soon end with the conclusion that since capitalism was born in a Europe that was still wholly Catholic, Catholics indisputably fostered its growth.

Instead, we interpret the facts—of which we propose to give a brief survey—in quite another manner.

Only unawares can Catholics truly conforming to their faith have favoured the development of capitalism —as understood in the sense we have already many times defined. Or else, only by consequences that humanly and practically could not be foreseen, could certain actions on the part of real and true Catholics have favoured capitalism. The bare enumeration of events will explain these statements.

It has been said by many that, first and foremost, the Popes encouraged capitalism inasmuch as they entrusted the collection of tithes and other dues to laymen. The spheres of activity of such laymen, it is said, were thus widened; during various periods of time they found themselves in possession of very large sums, and, directly or indirectly, they reaped large profits from their office as collectors. We have no reason to take exception to such a statement. Indeed, we may complete it by pointing out that the Popes, by entrusting the collection of dues to such laymen, encouraged them to travel in search of gain. Through these emissaries, protected by the apostolic authority, they facilitated the interrelation of markets and contributed to the cultural and spiritual formation of the great mediæval merchant and banking class.

The more we consider this fact, the greater its significance appears. For, again, the privileged position of these tithe-collectors, as men above the law, will have made them more likely to acquire the capitalistic mind, inasmuch as this demands detachment from the rules of the guilds and cities to which the majority of mediæval merchants were subject. It is on the spiritual consequences of such pontifical measures that we shall insist, though without forgetting their importance in respect of accumulation of capital. Besides allowing the merchants to handle such capital, the Popes put them in the way of making contacts and gaining an education through which they would become the founders of a capitalistically minded race. It was perhaps these collectors who, having these large sums at their disposal for a few days or at most a few months, first began to think of the value of time ; they were certainly the first to consider the question of risk, which they found so heavy, and the manner in which it could be shared. Another and important element in their education was the perils they had to meet among peoples who were always unwilling to part with money, even to St. Peter, and in countries of which the rulers, in every age, had they been able, would gladly have thrown the collectors into prison and taken their tributes for the royal treasuries.

But who would attribute such results to Catholicism ? And are those who would do so aware that in consequence they should give Catholicism the credit for having favoured the capitalistic development of the mining industry, simply because a Pope exploited to the full the alum mines of Tolfa ? Or for favouring capitalistic internationalism just because the Popes protected foreigners in the Middle Ages ?[1]   Then why not say, on far better grounds, that Catholicism favoured capitalistic finance, since the Popes permitted public debts, as exceptions to the prohibition of usury ? Or that Catholicism prepared the way for trusts and financial amalgamations, because, in the remote Middle Ages, its moralists advised contractors to form companies rather than have recourse to onerous loans ?

Moreover, once embarked upon this course, we find far more solid foundations for the assertion that Catholicism paved the way for the culminating aspiration of capitalism, a vast and unified market, by maintaining the unity of faith up to the sixteenth century ; by striving to restore political unity through its assistance to the new-born and never prosperous Holy Roman Empire of the West during the Middle Ages ; by gaining lost outlets for Europe, and the unity of the Mediterranean in the time of the Crusades ; by facilitating the progressive development of colonial policy through the Missions in modern times. And why should we forget the more modest yet no less effective work of the Abbots and Bishops, who, round about the abbeys and cities of the Middle Ages, protected the first markets, or became moneylenders ?[2]

---

[1] See G. P. Bognetti, *Note per la storia del passaporto e del salvacondotto*, Pavia, Treves, 1933.

[2] E. Allix and R. Genestal, " Les opérations financières de l'abbaye de Troarn du XI au XIV siècles " in *Vierteljahrschrift für Sozial- und Wirtschaftsgeschichte*, 1904, vol. II ; R. Genestal, *Rôle des monastères comme*

But then, we do not see why less attention should be paid to the efforts of those Catholics who, as Catholics, attacked low wages, since their struggle, by constraining employers to increase expenditure, drove them to develop machinery and hence to advance the conquests of capitalism. We have come now to a *reductio ad absurdum*—as we intended, so that it should be plain to all how mistaken it is, in considering the relations between capitalism and Catholicism, deliberately to pause at this or that fact, this or that measure, this or that action, for which, whatever its results, responsibility lies not with Catholicism as a doctrine, but with some individual Catholic, be he Pope or sacristan. Whoever the author of such acts may be, they have nothing to do with Catholicism, either because their author was not acting in conformity with Catholic teaching, or because they produced results which, had they been known to the author, would have prevented him from so acting so long as he wished to act in conformity with his faith.

If we now pass on to consider the action of Catholics who, as exponents of Catholicism, strove to replace arbitrary action by legality, disorder by order, oppression by freedom, we shall notice that even they helped to bring about situations from which capitalism drew strength ; just as they worked—and there is no need for

établissements de crédit étudié en Normandie du XI à la fin du XIII siècle, Paris, Rousseau, 1901. On the moneylending activities of the Templars, see H. Van der Linden, " Les Templiers à Louvain " in *Bulletin de l'Académie de Belgique*, 1923, p. 248.

157

us to give detailed examples—for an increasing protection of the interests of the individual in respect of economic exchanges, as against the interest of the State. But a detailed investigation of this kind would show us that the action of Catholics in this sense—inasmuch as they would be inspired by a special ideal of the ought-to-be, which, as we have already seen, does not coincide with the capitalistic ideal of the ought-to-be—favours capitalism up to a certain point, but in final analysis opposes it. Even apart from the pontifical prohibitions of the Middle Ages against trade with certain persons, infidels or otherwise[1]; apart from the obstacles set in the way of moneylenders and bankers by the establishment of *monts de piété* and rural savings banks, the fact remains that the Church, in the persons of her most authoritative exponents and her most devoted sons, fought against dawning capitalism, basing herself on the mediæval corporative order, and opposed triumphant capitalism, as we have seen, by calling upon the Social Catholics.

In the Middle Ages, by supporting the intervention of public bodies in economic life as a check to individual activity and to defend the interests of society as a whole; in our own time, by calling for State intervention for the same reasons, the Church has remained faithful to her

---

[1] It is well known how much such prohibitions injured various capitalistic groups. For example, during the War of the Eight Saints, after the papal excommunications " in many places, as in Paris, in England, in Flanders, in Germany and at Avignon, everywhere we were robbed, and no Florentine dared to stay in the said places " (G. Sercambi, *Croniche*, Parte I, c. CCLIV, vol. I, p. 216).

anti-capitalistic ethics. Both during the predominance of the mediæval guild system, and during that of capitalism, the Church, and those Catholics that listened to her voice, set or sought to set bounds not lawfully to be overstepped to the course of economic life—even at the cost of a sacrifice of mechanical and technical progress, which, in the Catholic conception of society, has never been identical with civilization.[1] It is in a diverse manner of conceiving all the values of life that Catholicism is opposed to capitalism, not as a complexus of instruments and means, but as an organization directing these means to a certain end. Catholicism finds no reason to object to mechanical looms or wireless. But so long as Catholicism remains Catholicism it can never accept a society like our own in which wireless and mechanical looms are the instruments for attaining quite other goals than those proposed by Catholicism.

Anyone who strives to understand exactly the respective positions of Catholicism and capitalism cannot be surprised to find the two ideals in conflict, and the exponents of the one contending with the exponents of the other for the domination of society.

It only remains for us to repeat that the Catholic *ethos* is anti-capitalistic; that Catholicism has opposed the establishment of capitalism, even if in certain ways it has favoured its progress in this or that direction.

[1] On p. 267 of his work, Groethuysen mentions the extreme views in a typical dispute between Catholics and capitalists on the nature of progress. The Catholics maintain that it is not bound up with the triumph of capitalism.

CHAPTER VI

THE RISE OF CAPITALISM

1. Capitalism in a Catholic age.   2. Reasons for its appearance.

1. IF Catholicism and Catholics did not pave the way
for the advent of capitalism, when and where did this
come about?   In Protestant countries after Luther's
revolt? Many declare that it flourished in such countries,
but as for its birth, no one now denies that it took place
before the Reformation, and hence in Catholic countries,
among Catholics. It is to explaining this fact, which,
after our statements in previous pages, may seem a
paradox, that we shall devote the present chapter, a
parenthesis in our wide survey of the influence of religion
on capitalism. A parenthesis, let us add, that is in no wise
useless, for, while we seek to discover the extra-religious
forces that brought about the first developments of
capitalism, we end by determining with ever greater
precision the part played by religious causes.

In Chapter III we recalled various capitalistic facts
to be found before the sixteenth century. Here, to
confine ourselves for the moment to Italy, we have to
recall that in the Italian cities of the fourteenth and
fifteenth centuries competition had become intense,
and beyond what was allowed by law. Masters already

160

use the truck system, in order to make the maximum profits by paying the minimum wage to their workers,[1] nor do they disdain to renounce a part of their freedom, imploring the new-born State for tariff measures to their advantage. There is also an unbridled speculation in loans—the lawfulness of which was once doubtful and debatable—on the part of men who take advantage of the needs or incompetence of their fellow-citizens.[2]

An attempt to diminish risk and increase profit is made by the new means of insurance, which develops considerably in Italy from the beginning of the fourteenth century.[3] To avoid the risk involved in transport of money, letters of exchange are invented[4] and largely used even for small payments.[5] Acquaintance with these instruments of commerce so develops that the rates of bank bills in Venice lead to wild speculation.[6] Old instruments of commerce are perfected, the bill of exchange, the draft, the bill of lading, are perfected between the fourteenth and fifteenth centuries, and are of great assistance to the increase in trade. Book-keeping becomes increasingly adequate to the needs of

---

[1] G. Sercambi, *Croniche*, Part II, Chap. CCLXXXVIII, vol. III, p. 252. The employers pay their spinners, dyers, etc., " in cloth, or worse things, counting a piece at four florins an ell which is not worth two."

[2] B. Barbadoro, *Le finanze della repubblica fiorentina*, Florence, Olschki, 1929, p. 606.

[3] G. Salvioli, *L'assicurazione ed il cambio marittimo nella storia del diritto italiano*, Bologna, Zanichelli, 1884, and E. Bensa, *Il contratto d'assicurazione nel Medioevo*, Genoa, Tip. Marittima, 1884.

[4] J. Thompson, *Economic and Social History of Europe*, New York, The Century Co., 1931, p. 438.

[5] E. Bensa, *Francesco di Marco*, op. cit., p. 353.

[6] R. Cessi, " La crisi economica veneziana del sec. XV " in *Economia*, July, 1923.

M

the time. Inventories, accounts, ledgers are kept, and there is even an attempt, in the first half of the fourteenth century, to establish a scientific system of industrial accountancy.[1] "We have before us," writes Bensa, " an evolution that takes possession, so to say, of all the more important commercial institutions existing in the fourteenth century, and which is a prelude to the complete transformation of commerce that has come about in modern times." [2]

If such a change took place in the form of business, the substance was not neglected. Work is speeded up ; all that is sought is the means that will produce the greatest profit. Traditional routes no longer satisfy, and efforts are made to find still better ways of transport, as we see, for instance, in the search for an easier way to India. In commercial policy there is an endeavour to reach the most profitable agreements, and even obstacles of a religious nature are set aside, as we see from the treaties with the Turks, or the substitution of a rational use of tribunals and arbitration for traditional reprisals, which destroyed everything. Individuals no longer feel their activity circumscribed by love of country ; they are ready to leave their country for ever if they can find a better field elsewhere for their business. In order to earn money, they devote themselves to every trade, and, since this is not enough, they go so far as to persuade their sons into the priesthood, their daughters

[1] Sapori, *Una compagnia*, etc., op. cit., pp. 255 et sq.
[2] E. Bensa, op. cit., p. 176.

into the convent, if in the first case they can acquire wealth and in the second save money. If expense can be saved by the employment of a slave, a slave is bought to take the place of the paid servant. If gambling leads to gain, men devote themselves to gambling, while civil legislation may either exploit or forbid it, and ecclesiastical legislation condemns it. If an increase of profits can only be obtained by enticing away the best workers from a rival, there is no longer hesitation in so doing.[1] Such are the actions performed by men whose lives are oriented in a capitalistic direction; they are performed because society no longer condemns but justifies them. Leon Battista Alberti justifies them in his book, *Libri della Famiglia*; Buonaccorso Pitti in his Chronicle boasts of prosperous transactions. Even attempts may be made to wring from rulers authorizations once unthinkable, as when, in 1468, Raffaele de' Neri, for 2,000 ducats, obtained from the Lord of Milan permission to hold a lottery.[2] Nor is the severity of ecclesiastical legislation a check. When in 1453 Cardinal Bessarion promulgated sumptuary laws, with a long Latin dissertation appealing to the examples of the ancients, Nicolosa Sanuti of Bologna protested against his measures, and tried, though unsuccessfully, to obtain their repeal.[3]

We could give further illustrations of this point if we were to repeat what we have already written in

[1] N. Rodolico, *Il popolo minuto*, Bologna, Zanichelli, 1899, p. 120.
[2] L. Zdekauer, *Sull'organizzazione del Giuoco*, op. cit., p. 79.
[3] L. Frati, op. cit., pp. 30–5.

Chapter III of an earlier work. But still better, a patient investigator, ready to consult mountains of documents, manuscript and printed, in order to see the successful or unsuccessful efforts of fifteenth-century Italians to modify the measures of public bodies in a capitalistic sense, would be able to prove that not only were there capitalistically minded men in Italy in that Catholic age, but also those who sought to obtain greater freedom of action by converting their contemporaries to their own way of thinking through alliance with the laws.

If this came about in the most progressive country in Europe,[1] France, England, Spain, Flanders, and certain parts of Germany were not backward in this respect.

To prove the existence of individuals moved by a capitalistic spirit in the Catholic England of the Middle Ages,[2] it is enough to recall the enclosure movement from the fourteenth century onwards, which transformed the country into a great producing country, first of wool, then of woollen fabrics, when the welcome and lucrative task of spinning and weaving the prized fleece of the English sheep was no longer left to foreigners across the Channel. The enclosure movement was so universal, and met with such opposition from the authorities and the peasants, but at the same time was so profitable,

[1] A complete picture of the capitalistic features of Italian economy between the fourteenth and the sixteenth centuries is to be found in G. Luzzatto, *Storia econ.*, op. cit., p. 148.

[2] According to Brodnitz (*Englische Wirtschaftgeschichte*, Jena, Fischer, 1918, Chap. XVI), the spirit of gain was potent in England before the Reformation, and the breach with traditionalism had already come about. See also A. Fanfani, *Scisma e spirito capitalistico in Inghilterra*, Milan, Rovida e Gadda, 1932.

that in itself it suffices to show that those responsible for it were not only completely detached from the dictates of cultural and social tradition, but had the courage to face the risks of the international market and to defy the wrath of the peasants and of the law, all solely for the love of gain.

But side by side with the sheep breeders, well before the Reformation, manufacturers and merchants showed themselves to possess the particular spirit that marks the business man. In proof of this we find the statement of the Ypres magistrates, who in 1445 declared that English competition had destroyed the weaving industry in that city,[1] and the remarkable and growing number of pieces of cloth exported,[2] which is such that we are not surprised to discover the existence at the beginning of the sixteenth century of many of those great woollen factories of which that of John Withcombe is an imposing prototype.[3] A Bishop of the fifteenth century has a forge, which, in respect of the organization of labour, has now a definitely capitalistic significance, while merchants begin to control considerable tonnage for maritime transport.[4] We must note also that a pre-capitalist spirit has ceased to regulate

[1] H. Pirenne, *Les dénombrements de la population*, etc., art. quoted, p. 6.
[2] R. H. Tawney, *The Agrarian Problem in the Sixteenth Century*, London, Longmans, 1912, p. 196.
[3] P. Mantoux, *The Industrial Revolution in the Eighteenth Century*, London, 1929, pp. 33–5.
[4] William Canynges, of Bristol, in 1461 had ten ships, and John Taverner, of Hull, in 1449 built a large carrack on the measurements of the most powerful vessels of Genoa and Venice (H. Meredith, *Outlines of the Economic History of England*, London, Pitman, p. 135).

the lives of those peasants who seek to send their sons into the towns to learn a trade, or weavers who, in order to escape the rigorous and onerous control of the guilds, leave the towns and set up manufactures in the suburbs.

Such men, as in Italy, try on several occasions to influence national policy in their own interests, either by opposing the concession of privileges to foreigners [1] or hampering the foreign policy of the sovereign. When in 1528 England allied herself with France as a step to war with the Emperor, there was a general protest throughout the kingdom. The Kent cloth makers, seeing their business with Flanders threatened, plotted to murder Wolsey, who supported the war. The Wiltshire weavers were on the verge of revolt. [2] The rulers themselves, in 1503, have to note " that men "—to use Cunningham's words—" were seeking their private lucre and singular advantage, without having due care for the prosperity of the community. Artisans who withdrew from the pressure of burgh rates and the restrictions of craft guilds, landlords who raised their rents, miners who did their work in the easiest way," without caring whether their operations silted up the

---

[1] J. Mazzei, *Politica economica inter. inglese prima di A. Smith*, op. cit., pp. 9–10 ; W. Cunningham, *The Growth of English Industry and Commerce during the Early and Middle Ages*, 5th ed., Cambridge University Press, 1927, p. 291 ; E. Lipson, *The Economic History*, etc., vol. I, pp. 451 sq. According to Beardwood's recent research (*Alien Merchants in England, 1350 to 1377*, Cambridge, Mass., Mediæval Academy of America, 1931), foreigners were not really granted privileges, but only a parity of rights with natives. This indeed, in view of mediæval legislation on foreigners, may appear as privileged treatment.

[2] G. Constant, *La Réforme en Angleterre*, op. cit., p. 65.

ports of Plymouth, Dartmouth, Fowey, Falmouth, " were all branded as victims of covetousness." [1]

We have referred particularly to Italy and England for two different reasons : the former was undoubtedly the most economically advanced country of the Middle Ages; the latter, though the least advanced, was destined to be in the forefront of capitalist nations, and this many have attributed to the effects of the Reformation. And if in England, in a country in the Middle Ages more backward than Germany, we find the promising seeds of an initial capitalism, it seems to us needless to produce at equal length the results of our research in respect of the Germanic countries, in which, while the quays of the Hanseatic cities show notable signs of incipient commercial capitalism,[2] there is such economic development that, in comparison, the following centuries will appear as decadence.[3] The metal industry of Nürnberg becomes world famous; the merchants procure like fame for Augsburg and Ravensburg.[4] The German bourgeoisie of the Middle Ages produces champions of early capitalism, who are universally recognized, and who derive no few advantages from the capitalistically organized mining industry,[5] which is the real basis of the economy of their land.

---

[1] W. Cunningham, *The Growth* . . . , op. cit., pp. 480 et sq.

[2] E. Daenell, *Die Blütezeit der deutschen Hanse*, 2 vols., Berlin, G. Reimer, 1905–6; F. Roerig, op. cit., loc. cit.

[3] G. Luzzatto, *Storia econ.*, op. cit., pp. 208–16.

[4] A. Schulte, *Geschichte der grossen Ravensburger Handelsgesellschaft* (1380–1530), 3 vols., Stuttgart-Berlin, Deutsche Verlags-Anstalt, 1923.

[5] J. Strieder, *Die Deutsche Montan- und Metall-industrie im Zeitalter der Fugger*, Berlin, Verlag, G. M. B. H., 1931, pp. 34–8.

Exploiting every combination of circumstances, the Welser, Tucher, Imhof, Humpis, Hochstetter, Baumgarten, Fugger,[1] achieve a success that, if it testifies to their tenacity and good fortune, testifies also to capitalistic developments in an age that either preceded the Reformation or came so soon after that its spiritual results, necessarily slow, were not yet felt.

Certainly we shall not be able to quote Flanders as an example of the influence of the Reformation on the development of capitalism, for it is well known that as a result of various factors, the Netherlands actually declined in the sixteenth century, whereas in the fifteenth they had been acquainted with such a definitely capitalistic phenomenon as the migration of industries from the towns to the country in order to avoid guild restrictions,[2] and at the same time had seen the cloth merchant assume the role of the modern capitalist employer.[3] While the Flemish ports were of such importance that the Venetian galleys braved the ocean in order to call there.[4]

Nor was France behindhand in comparison with the countries we have mentioned. In France, had there been no spontaneous native manifestations of capitalism,[5] these would have been produced by the host of Italian

---

[1] A. Schulte, op. cit. ; R. Ehrenberg, op. cit ; Haebler, *Die überseeischen Unternehmungen der Welser*, Leipzig, 1903.

[2] L. Dechesne, *Histoire économique et sociale*, op. cit., pp. 149–52.

[3] G. Des Marez, *L'organisation du travail à Bruxelles au XV siècle*, Bruxelles, Lamertin, 1904, Chap. IV.

[4] R. Cessi, " Le relazioni commerciali fra Venezia e le Fiandre nel secolo XIV " in *Nuovo Archivio Veneto*, new series, year XIV (1914), vol. XXVII, part I, passim.

[5] See Henri Hauser in *Les débuts du capitalisme*.

merchants who, from the eleventh century onwards, crossed the Savoyard Alps and "began to lend money and carry on usury in France and elsewhere beyond the mountains, where they made much money,"[1] or who landed on the shores of Provence and made their way up the Rhone valleys, overran the hills of Champagne, invaded the plains of Flanders, and from the Atlantic coasts set sail for England. It would seem that the Italians found apt pupils in their cousins beyond the Alps, if these became their rivals in the eastern markets, made Marseilles a port rivalling the ports of Italy,[2] and produced that Jacques Cœur who had no reason to envy the most famous "Lombards."[3] Soon the Languedoc dyers had learned to dye their stuffs with Barbary aniline and Portingade indigo, which, while it profited the producer, injured the purchaser, for the acid burned the cloth.[4] Following in the footsteps of the Bardi, Peruzzi, and Medici, the Dinant merchants in 1465 sent their goods to England "to make profit or to advance themselves, since every merchant seeks his profit and advancement." But better than in any words of ours we find the capitalistic attitude of the French merchants defined in a petition to the Hanseatic League in 1487. It contains these words: "*cum unusquique mercator ad unum finem tendat ut facultates suas aug-*

---

[1] *Chronicon Astense*, in Rerum Ital. Script., vol. XI, p. 142.
[2] H. Scherer, "Storia del commercio di tutte le nazioni da' tempi antichi fino a' nostri giorni" in *Biblioteca dell'economista*, series II, vol. IV, Turin, Utet, 1864, pp. 192–3.
[3] R. Bouvier, op. cit.
[4] G. Faignez, op. cit., p. 378.

mentet, competentiora et aptiora que potest media investigat ut ad eum finem intendat." [1]

The Italians fostered the capitalistic spirit in the trade of cloth and money, the English in the woollen trade, the Flemish in linen, the Hanseatic towns in the redistribution of spices among the northern countries. Among the French there were those who enriched themselves and intensified their capitalistic instincts in the international wine trade,[2] while " everyone goes in for business," as Claude de Seyssel bore witness in 1515.[3] Thus in the Catholic Middle Ages the whole of Western Europe, including Spain, where international trade on a large scale, with the use of highly perfected methods, the bill of lading, and insurance, was not unknown, saw the rise of great numbers of early capitalists ; saw them at work, intent on evading the constraint of the laws and on procuring privileges from the princes.

This fact makes us ask ourselves if it be indeed true that Catholicism always opposed the capitalistic spirit as it revealed itself in a Catholic age, and what forces supported it in its first manifestations.

2. Since we find that capitalism first arose in a pre-capitalistic world, we can only suppose that there were certain practical circumstances that induced certain individuals to adopt a mode of action at variance with

[1] Pirenne, *Les Marchands,* op. cit., p. 447.
[2] H. Pirenne, " Un grand commerce d'exportation au Moyen Age : les vins de France " in *Annales d'histoire économique et sociale,* 1933, p. 8.
[3] F. Bezold, *L'età della Riforma,* Venice, " La nuova Italia editrice," p. 156.

that of the majority of their contemporaries and with what should have been the mode of action of all.[1] We must also suppose that there were also circumstances of a moral order such that not only did those who so acted feel no incentive to return to legal methods, but were encouraged to persist in their abnormal course in the conviction that theirs was the right path; so that, from erring individuals, they became apostles of a new mode of thought and life.

We have taken this twofold supposition as our guide in explaining the rise of the capitalist spirit and of resulting capitalistic actions, in a society which, imbued with the Catholic social ideal, found itself at the opposite pole to the capitalistic conception.

While the Catholic conception was firmly established in individuals, it also informed public institutions, and these became its defence. So long as the capitalistically minded were isolated individuals, operating where the law was or could be enforced, they could depart little, or only for brief periods, from pre-capitalist normality. They needed opportunities which would make it easier for them to infringe the prevailing code, induce them to repeat such infringements, and put them under necessity of perpetuating them.[2] These opportunities, which

[1] Robertson (op. cit., Chap. III) seeks to prove that the capitalistic spirit, taken as economic individualism, sprang from practical life and was an aspiration characteristic of the merchants and not yet of the philosophers.

[2] Luzzatto (*Storia econ.*, op. cit., p. 68) writes that " no sooner did a city begin to break through the narrow circle that had hitherto circumscribed its life and the horizons of its citizens, no sooner did some of these dare the risks of trade in far countries, where they found wholly new opportunities of gain,

presented themselves in ever greater numbers with the increase of large-scale commerce,[1] and later with the extension of the market consequent on geographical discovery,[2] a man would more easily find in other countries than his own. There the laws had less force for him ; as a foreigner, exposed to a special supervision and treated almost as an enemy, he felt himself almost justified in a revolt that in his own country he would never have attempted, even apart from legal prohibitions. Faced with foreign customers, the merchant is withheld from pushing competitive methods to their extreme limit only by the power of the law. He is not held back by all the motives of a sentimental order that, in his own country, where every customer was an acquaintance and in a measure a judge, would have constrained him to remain within the bounds of legality even when he was sure of impunity.[3] In a place visited for the first and last time, there is certainly a smaller incentive to correct behaviour than in a man's own town, where every eye will bear witness against him his life through, and every accusing tongue will find ready ears. And, again, for a man to leave his country for purposes of trade means to expose himself to greater risks, which cannot be

where their audacity opens new horizons to the produce of the city, bringing about the growth of industry for export, than the doctrine of the just mean, of blessed mediocrity, loses all its force."

[1] G. Luzzatto, op. cit., pp. 59–63.
[2] H. Robertson, op. cit., pp. 176–7.
[3] W. Sombart, *Der mod. Kapit.*, op. cit., vol. I, Chap. LXI ; R. J. Lemoine, *Les étrangers et la formation du capitalisme*, art. cit. On the economic virtues of the foreign immigrants in England, after the Reformation, see E. Levy, op. cit., pp. 46 and 69–70.

foreseen and may vary from moment to moment. It is easy to imagine how the fear of losing his capital from one moment to another may affect a man who is set on achieving a definite amount of profit. If it is true that the conduct of the capitalist to-day is dominated and governed by the pressure of risk, it is easy to deduce that one of the most potent factors in turning man away from the paths of pre-capitalism was risk, the fear of loss. The graver and more insistent the risk, the more insistent and decided became his effort to evade it, even at the price of repudiating his loyalty to a pre-capitalist ideal. And if in the presence of fierce, ever increasing, and unbridled competition—no longer restrained by law, for the very man who has to defend himself against such competition has brought about the abrogation of the law—risk ceases to be a force operating only in a few international markets, but operates in all markets, even in those provided by obscure country towns, it is easy to understand that the incentive to act in a capitalistic manner will become universal. To act, that is, in order to obtain the maximum, momentary personal economic profit—a profit momentary because, given the perils that threaten, no one can tell what he will gain on the morrow.

The pressure of risk leads the individual to place all his hopes not in a series of productive acts, but in the first alone. Just as a State that ran grave risk of being unable to collect taxes on any but a single day in the year would not spread the collection over three hundred

173

and sixty-five days, but would try to get in as much as possible on the given day.

Religious and civil precepts were less resolute in opposing such efforts to guard against the dangers of risk when the merchant was confronted with men of another religion, or with those with whom his country was at war. In such moments the mediæval mentality itself[1] came to the support of innate aspirations to profit, and encouraged the trader to enrich himself under a pretext of religion or patriotism. The expansion of trade worked in the same sense, when, summoning a man forth from the walls of his city, and bringing him into contact with men to whom he felt himself in no way bound, it encouraged an unbridled and irregular thirst for gain.[2] Those difficulties and changes in social custom that we have frequently mentioned, and the bitterness of party struggles, had a like result.[3] Famines, wars, frequent sieges, by increasing risk and opportunities of unexpected gains, must have played a considerable part in arousing a mercenary instinct. Toniolo[4] held indeed that certain of the characteristics of the capitalist spirit (thirst for gain and cosmopolitanism) were the result of technical developments. In reality, the relationship is mutual, although it cannot be denied that

---

[1] The laws allowed infidel enemies to be sold into slavery and exploited ; piratical raids and the despoiling of men and peoples under the ban of Christendom were also lawful.

[2] C. Supino, *Il desiderio del lucro*, Bocca, Turin, 1905, p. 8.

[3] Caggese (*Firenze dalla decadenza di Roma al Risorgimento d'Italia*, Florence, Seeber-Bemporad, 1912 et sq., vol. II, p. 8) points out that party hatred opened the way to commercial competition among citizens of one city.

[4] G. Toniolo, *Trattato di econ. sociale*, op. cit., vol. I, p. 302.

technical development, inasmuch as it brought about the creation of huge agglomerations of interests and mass production, increased the pressure of risk and thus increased capitalistic cosmopolitanism and thirst for gain. But what is true of an advanced stage of technical progress is not true for its beginnings. We prefer the view that it was the capitalistic spirit with its thirst for gain that led to a quest for technical improvements, or to the utilization of inventions made from other motives.

Those who have followed our argument cannot fail to conclude, as we do, that in the Middle Ages it was the international trade ventures that did most to favour the rise of the capitalist spirit. In the light of these considerations, the conception of trade in St. Thomas, the champion of the Catholic social ideal, appears only logical, " For," says St. Thomas, " the city that for its subsistence has need of much merchandise must necessarily submit to the presence of foreigners. Now relations with foreigners, as Aristotle says in his *Politics*, very often corrupt national customs : the foreigners who have been brought up under other laws and customs, in many cases act otherwise than is the use of the citizens, who, led by their example, imitate them and so bring disturbance into social life. Moreover, if the citizens themselves engage in commerce, they open the way to many vices. For since the aim of merchants is wholly one of gain, greed takes root in the heart of the citizens, by which everything, in the city, becomes venal, and, with the disappearance of good faith, the way is open to

175

fraud; the general good is despised, and each man will seek his own particular advantage; the taste for virtue will be lost when the honour which is normally the reward of virtue is accorded to all. Hence, in such a city civil life cannot fail to grow corrupt." [1]

When these words are understood, and we bear in mind the ideal of a Catholic society and the aspirations of capitalism, we can easily see why the friar noted a tendency to reason only in a " venal " manner and (" despising the general good ") to seek only " particular advantage."

The characteristics of capitalism are precisely the following: the adoption of an economic criterion as criterion of order; failure to consider third persons; a quest for purely individual profit. Nor did Aquinas exaggerate when he saw in the merchant the greatest danger to " civil life," as he understood it. It is not by chance that the first capitalistic figures presented to us are merchants—Godric, later St. Godric, presented by Pirenne; the Mairano by Heynen; the Bardi, the Peruzzi, the Del Bene by Sapori; Datini by Bensa; the Fugger by Strieder. Nor is it by chance that though opinions differ as to whether capitalism sprang from land-owners or traders, all agree that even land-owners first showed themselves capitalistic in the quality of merchants. [2] In

---

[1] St. Thomas, *De Reg. princ.*, Book II, Chap. III.

[2] In a work we are preparing on economic life in the Italian country districts in the fourteenth century, we are able to show how in a certain region of Italy it was the traders, newly come into capital, who transformed themselves into land-owners, and not the land-owners into traders.

mediæval economic society the only individual who could easily and often find himself in a position to act otherwise than in conformity with pre-capitalist economic ideals was the merchant.[1] Having left his city, exposed to risks of every kind, free from such ties as the laws of his country or the opinions of his acquaintances, surrounded by intriguing people who saw in him only someone to be cheated, he had to defend himself against the cheaters by cheating, against competitors by sharpening his wits to find new methods of competition, and against adverse circumstances by learning to overcome them. Although he may have been a God-fearing man, if it was urgent for him to take back to the warehouse at least the equivalent of what he had brought away, he was obliged to throw overboard something of his pre-capitalistic ideas, even if in paradisal conditions they might have appealed to him.

In another part of the present work we have pointed out that in a pre-capitalist society if a single individual breaks away from the norm, the others will be forced to follow his example if only in self-defence. Let the reader then consider the vast significance of encounters either with merchants of another religion, or with subtle, equivocal, and unscrupulous merchants, always ready to take advantage of any opportunity. Faced with these, men's faithfulness to their own ideals will have

---

[1] On the spirit of the great mediæval merchant, see the conclusion of Luzzatto's study : *Piccoli e grandi mercanti nelle città italiane del Rinascimento,* in the volume of essays in honour of Prof. Giuseppe Prato (Turin, R. Istituto Superiore di Scienze Economiche e Commerciali, 1930).

begun to waver; their consequent actions will have produced such remarkable results that we doubt whether their conviction of wrong-doing will have been reinforced. To reason in terms of utility means a tangible result; to reason in terms of Paradise means hope of a result of which the certainty vanishes if faith weakens. We must not forget how much the capitalistic ideal has the advantage in being concrete, and, remembering this, we can more easily understand how a profitable infraction of pre-capitalist normality would rather lead men to repeat such infractions than arouse in them such remorse as to lead them back to the old path. We hold it a very significant fact that among mediæval merchants remorse led to notable conversions even when in no danger of death. It is enough to quote St. Godric, St. Francis, Blessed Colombini. It led also to death-bed restitutions, often complete, and which were the more wonderful the harder it had been for the dying man to scrape together his hoard, and the more reluctant he had been in life to give a penny to anyone who had not earned it twice over.[1] Such conversions, implying a return to pre-capitalistic modes of life, continue so long as there is faith, but when faith weakens there is no longer thought of reparation.

It is the waning of faith that explains the establishment of a capitalistic spirit in a Catholic world, but in a certain sense it is the establishment of the capitalistic spirit

---

[1] See A. Fanfani, *Le origini dello spir.*, pp. 50 sq. On the magnitude of testamentary alms, see A. Fanfani, " I benefattori di una fraternita toscana " in *Aevum*, No. 4, October-December, 1933.

that brings about a waning of faith.[1] The effect of the weakening of faith is that the material factors we have mentioned change from momentary circumstances to permanent ones. With the weakening of faith remorse becomes rare; the " is " is no longer compared with the " should-be," and that which is is accepted and exploited in accordance with its own standards; the world is judged by purely worldly criteria.

All the circumstances that, in the Middle Ages, led to a waning of faith explain the progressive establishment of the capitalistic spirit, for the pre-capitalist spirit rests on facts that are not seen, but must be held by faith. Those faithful to it sacrifice a certain result for a result that is guaranteed by faith ; they eschew a certain mode of action in the certainty of losing riches, but believing that they will gain a future reward in heaven. Let man lose this belief, and nothing remains for him, rationally speaking, but to act in a capitalistic manner. If there are no longer religious ties uniting man to man, there will be a growing number of audacious men whose sole end, in the words of Villari, is to be ahead of their fellows.[2] Such men existed before the modern era began, and of

---

[1] B. Groethuysen, op. cit., p. 59. " It is precisely in the discord between Christian and bourgeois life, between the old man and the new man, that we must seek the cause of bourgeois incredulity. How could a man continue to believe in mysteries, in legends, in miracles, when his every effort went to eliminating all that was irrational from his life ? How could he continue to recognize Divine Providence, and how could he continue convinced that the will of God governs everything, when a confidence in his own strength and a reasoned foresight are the motives inspiring all his reasoning ? "
[2] P. Villari, *Niccolò Machiavelli e i suoi tempi*, Milan, Hoepli, 4th ed., 1927, vol. I, p. 23.

such men it has been said that they showed "a complete lack of scruples and contempt for every moral law."[1]

Men were particularly encouraged to sharpen their wits to acquire wealth, and moral obstacles were removed by the fact that, by a subversion of ancient custom, the highest offices no longer fell to those summoned to them by law or custom, but to those who could win them either by their own or others' wit, by their own or others' material strength, or by their own ability and others' baseness. In each case the stair of ascent was provided by economic means, from the moment that economic difficulties made all feel the need of goods. The Emperor no longer sought homage but money, the Cities widened their domains more by gold than by arms. Bankers became masters of cities without striking a blow. Gold paved the way and opened the gates to the new tyrants. Even the man who, from lofty motives, had no need of money could not do without it, if he did not wish to cut a poor figure at banquets and ceremonies, or be behindhand in public largesse.

It is a vicious circle. A man seeks goods because he no longer believes in a faith that bounded his desires, and he no longer believes because he has experienced the pleasures of possession and influence. We need not enquire at what moment the former or the latter of these causes came into operation; we know that their working

[1] P. Boissonnade, *Le Travail dans l'Europe Chrétienne au Moyen Age*, Paris, Alcan, 1921, p. 374.

varied from country to country, from individual to
individual, and that now a man might be tempted to
discount morality by the attraction of goods, and now
might be tempted to enrich himself because he no longer
believed in divine penalties and rewards. And if in the
case of an individual it would be hard to say which
cause came first, it would be impossible in the case of
society. We may take it for granted that in society as
a whole both causes worked simultaneously, each
stimulated by the other.

There were other phenomena that encouraged either
acquisitive action or incredulity. Leaving aside the
less important and local ones, and confining ourselves
to those of which the action was most general at the
close of the pre-capitalist period, we may say that the
greatest contribution to the new economic spirit informing fifteenth-century men was brought by the humanist
conception of life, of which the exponents, such as
Alberti, took the most significant step towards the
capitalist spirit by detaching their conception of wealth
from its moral setting, and withdrawing the acquisition
and use of goods from the influence of the rules and
restrictions of religious morality.[1] The advent of similar
tendencies in the political field [2] had the result that the
State ceased to oppose the new mode of thought and
life, and instead itself threw off the influence of Catholic

[1] Cf. Chap. V of the work by the present author, already quoted.
[2] C. Curcio, *La politica italiana del '400*, Florence, " Nuovissima," 1932,
p. 14.

ideals, often in order to exploit human vices, as we see in legislation on gambling.[1]

All these reasons explain the fact that the birth, and early, by no means inconsiderable, manifestations of the capitalist spirit took place in a Catholic world. In this same period many other circumstances combined to provoke technical developments, but these, though they served the capitalist spirit, as means serve an idea, have nothing to do with it. We have already drawn a clear distinction between capitalism and mechanism, hence between capitalism and technical methods, though noting that capitalistic ambitions gave a considerable impetus to technical progress. But just as no one identifies war with the manufacture of arms, which owes its progress to war, no one can identify mechanical and technical methods, the instruments of production, with capitalism, which instead exerts its greatest influence in the sphere of social and economic organization. In this way it encourages technical progress in order to fill in gaps and perfect productive processes.

For these reasons, we shall not here enquire into the circumstances that stimulated technical improvements before the Reformation, though we would point out that certain such improvements there were, especially in regard to circulation of money. But it should not be forgotten that in respect of these, capitalistic ideals reinforced the stimulus of outward circumstances.

[1] L. Zdekauer, " Il gioco in Italia nei secoli XIII e XIV e specialmente a Firenze " in *Archivio Storico Italiano*, IV, vol. XVIII, 1886.

CHAPTER VII

PROTESTANTISM AND CAPITALISM

1. Economic and social effects of the Reformation. 2. Protestant moralists and economic problems. 3. Protestantism and capitalism. 4. Problem of the predominantly capitalistic development of Protestant countries.

1. OUR investigations have led us to the conclusion—which is now shared even by those historians whose conceptions of capitalism differ from our own—that Europe was acquainted with capitalism before the Protestant revolt. For at least a century capitalism had been an ever growing collective force. Not only isolated individuals, but whole social groups, inspired with the new spirit, struggled with a society that was not yet permeated with it.

Once we have ruled out that Protestantism could have produced a phenomenon that already existed, it still remains for us to enquire whether capitalism was encouraged or opposed by Protestantism. Such encouragement or opposition could result either from events to which the Protestant movement gave rise, or from doctrines implicit in Protestant ideology.

The Reformation led to so many events, which had such far-reaching consequences, that it is not hard to

183

pick out at least a few that encouraged capitalistic progress. This naturally did not come about in Italy or Spain, or in the countries that raised barriers to the spread of the new doctrine, though even these ended by feeling the effects of the revolution in thought. But it came about in the lands where Protestantism was able to establish itself, and especially in those where prevailing conditions were propitious to an expansion of economic life in a capitalistic direction.

Leaving out of account the anti-slavery movement[1] and the economic effects of the Wars of Religion,[2] we may say that the religious revolution was able to produce results of most universal consequence where it first took possession of the State. In no European country did this come about more swiftly than in Catholic England, where the revolt against Rome, at first merely schismatic, was the work of the King. In England, more completely than in any other country, the revolutionary changes entailed by heresy following on schism led to confiscation of church property, sale of lands, speculation, a reshifting of classes, an influx from lower to higher strata of society, and the advent of new plutocrats, new land-owners, new rulers.[3] The very vagueness of

[1] After Fox and his Quakers had denounced slavery, John Wesley, in 1774, launched his *Thoughts on Slavery*, which mark the beginning of an intensive anti-slavery campaign on the part of the Wesleyans (J. Warner, *The Wesleyan Movement in the Industrial Revolution*, London, Longmans, 1930, pp. 41–3).
[2] R. Ehrenberg, *Das Zeitalter der Fugger*, Jena, Fischer, 3rd ed., 1922, vol. II, pp. 178 et sq.
[3] S. B. Liljegren, *The Fall of the Monasteries and the Social Changes in England leading up to the Great Revolution*, Lund, C. Gleerup, 1924. Certain

184

the official form of the heresy led to doctrinal confusion which had its effects on practical life. The weakening of doctrinal guidance exasperated an egotism which had already received considerable stimulus from the system of confiscations, when the royal authority had set so great an example of contempt for established rights.

Moreover, confiscation encouraged speculation and a revival of the enclosure movement, which legal prohibitions were impotent to check.[1] We learn, too, from Nef's[2] researches that one effect of the confiscation of church property was the transfer of coal-bearing lands from the monks, who were conservative in method and none too expert, to laymen ready for innovations; hence a considerable stimulus to the coal industry. In other countries, such as Germany, and, later, Scandinavia,[3] there were confiscations, but if these did not lead to the same results as in England, this was due to the different political and economic situation in such countries, and, in Germany in particular, the destructive process was less complete.

It has been said by various authors that Protestantism encouraged the spread of capitalism by the migrations of its persecuted followers. In support of this thesis, it has been pointed out that the Flemish Reformers and

---

exaggerated conclusions are criticized by the present writer in an essay: "Alcune conseguenze economiche dei provvedimenti eversivi di Enrico VIII" in *Rivista Internazionale di Scienze Sociali*, July, 1932, with bibliography. See also J. Kraus, op. cit., p. 100.

[1] A. Fanfani, *Scisma e spirito capitalistico in Inghilterra.*
[2] J. U. Nef, op. cit., vol. I, pp. 133–56.
[3] H. Koht, *Les luttes des paysans en Norvège*, Paris, Payot, 1929, pp. 56–7.

Huguenots introduced the art of fine weaving into England, and the religious exiles from Locarno and Bergamo established new branches of the textile industry in Zurich and Bâle. According to Voltaire, the Huguenots in Germany peopled the towns, introduced the cloth and hat industry,[1] and reclaimed the Mark of Brandenburg. Others have noted how the Protestant colonies, by their thrifty spirit and untiring industry,[2] speedily accumulated capital, which assuredly encouraged the expansion of economic life in their new country. These facts are perfectly true, but are in no way connected with the religion of the social groups concerned. For even if it were true that their particular religious ethos encouraged such exiles in industry and thrift,[3] it is also true that such virtues are characteristic of all foreign groups in new countries. This has been shown by various researches into the effect of foreigners on the economic life of countries receiving them. It may be objected that none the less these exiles were such on account of their religion, but this argument, if it led anywhere, would lead to the absurdity of attributing the effects of such enforced exile, not indeed to the religion of the persecuted, but to the measures taken by their persecutors.

On these lines there is therefore little to say of the influence of Protestantism, as a religion, on capitalism.

---

[1] Voltaire, *Siècle de Louis XIV*, Paris, Diderot, 1864, p. 419.
[2] E. Rota, " Quel che la Germania deve alla Francia " in *Rivista delle nazioni latine*, December, 1918, p. 323.
[3] H. Levy, *Der Wirtschaftsliber.*, op. cit., p. 12.

We should rather ask whether these exiles, by their economic virtues and their technical knowledge, did not increase competition in their new countries, and thus expose themselves and their hosts to an increased risk, for to our mind risk is a most important factor in determining a capitalistic mode of action. It might also be said that any emigration, but especially that produced by religious persecution, means a spiritual cleavage from the persecuting fatherland, and hence fosters in the emigrants an internationalism that is no small element in capitalist mentality. And, again, we might ask whether these exiles, persecuted in their own countries, viewed with suspicion in their new ones [1]—as Levy has shown in respect of England—as a result of their misfortunes did not become the most fervent apostles of religious toleration and freedom—a fact of immense importance for the expansion of business, and highly prized by the capitalist.[2] It is indisputable that Protestantism, by immigration and otherwise, destroyed the unity of the State in the religious sphere and made its restoration impossible, so that King and subjects were faced with the problem of shelving the religious question in order to obtain such unity. Protestantism thus obliged the States to face the problem of freedom of conscience,

---

[1] H. Levy, op. cit., pp. 8-10.

[2] It should be noted that in the eighteenth century it is among the Protestants of America that we find the first to draw attention to the benefits of freedom. Adrian van der Donck says that the wealth of New Holland depended on freedom, and that any restriction of " individual gain or private trade " led to economic decadence (*Representation of New Netherlands*, p. 39. Similar considerations are to be found in W. Brandfort, on pp. 162 and 201 of his *Of Plimouth Plantation*).

which, advocated by authoritative Protestants,[1] once solved, meant the removal of an obstacle to economic life and encouraged the tendency to count the religious question among problems that could be left out of reckoning. From that time forth the State became more favourably disposed towards capitalism; it had no longer a creed to defend, but only interests, and in this sphere it was not hard to reach an understanding.

Protestantism, where it was represented by a minority or wherever it had the sovereign against it, encouraged the rise of a sentiment that is wholly modern, even if it was not unknown to some or other mediæval politician. It presented subjects with the problem of whether they were the State or whether the sovereign was the State; of whether their policy, interests, and will should prevail, or that of their sovereign.[2] It does not take much reflection to see the immense importance of even the raising of such a problem in regard to capitalistic aims. The moment it was raised, in view of the struggle to obtain possession of the State, efforts would be made by the capitalistically minded to make the interests defended

[1] Such were Milton, Locke and Cromwell. The last named expressed his thought clearly when he wrote: " The State, in choosing men to serve it, takes no notice of their opinions; if they be willing faithfull to serve it, that satisfies " (O. Cromwell, *Letters*, ed. Tauchnitz, Part II, letter 20, 10th March, 1643). For French advocates of toleration, see Mornet, op. cit., p. 23.

[2] The first experiment in this sense was that of the Peasants' Revolt in Germany, when the peasants claimed against the King a pretended divine right to pay lower taxes and render lighter services. This was the first result that though not " directly produced by the supreme leaders of the Reformation, was indisputably a consequence of the Reformation, albeit an unwished-for consequence " (K. Kaser, *Riforma e controriforma*, It. tr., Florence, Vallecchi, 1927, p. 38).

188

by the State coincide with their own, which they idealized to appear as the interests of civilization. The final victories in this struggle would be provided by parliamentary régimes and democratic systems, which, as Weber has shown, found full justification in the idea, peculiar to the Calvinistic groups, that creatures must not be glorified or accorded any differential treatment.[1]

It has been said that the Quakers, too, helped to pave the way for the advent of democratic systems, inasmuch as at their meetings they maintained the principle of the absolute equality of all,[2] while in formulating the duties entailed by wealth they paid no attention to those differences of class and social rank that received such importance in the teachings of the Catholic moralists.[3]

[1] On the importance of Puritanism in respect of the growth of democratic ideals, see M. James, *Social Problems and Policy during the Puritan Revolution*, London, Routledge, 1930, p. 340. The idea is by no means new, and was put forward several years earlier by E. Troeltsch, *Protestantism and the Formation of the Modern World*, op. cit., and E. Giovanetti, *Il tramonto del liberalismo*, Bari, Laterza, 1917, pp. xviii and 35.

We must, nevertheless, not forget that the idea of predestination has been judged as being by nature anti-equalitarian (R. Gonnard, *Histoire des doctrines économiques*, pp. 662–3) and that in Geneva the Calvinists by their sumptuary laws maintained a clear distinction between the classes (E. Troeltsch, *Die Soziallehren*, pp. 656 and 964). On the relations between the practice of primitive Calvinism and incipient democracy, cf. G. De Ruggiero, *Storia del liberalismo*, p. 17.

[2] I. Grubb, *Quakerism and Industry before 1800*, London, Williams and Norgate, p. 177.

[3] In Quaker addresses on simplicity of manners concern for equality reaches such a pitch that a direct appeal is made to the producer to refrain from producing luxury articles (I. Grubb, op. cit., Chap. VI). This shows the ideal of a society in which all would be on the same footing in regard to dress. Now while Catholics also recommend simplicity of manners, we find in Catholic preaching a constant anxiety to relate such simplicity to social distinctions, so that even one of the most rigid of Catholic moralists, Savonarola (*Della simplicità della vita cristiana*, Florence, Lib. Ed. Fiorentina, 1925, Book III, p. 63 and pp. 69–70), allows that the style and richness of a dress should correspond to the social rank of the wearer.

On the other hand, the followers of John Wesley did not encourage the advent of representative government, since, faithful to their master's declaration : " We are no republicans and never intend to be,"[1] they find moral, practical, and theological reasons[2] with which to refute the doctrine of parliamentary government.

2. That Protestantism in the ways we have mentioned exercised a positive influence in paving the way for the establishment of capitalism seems indisputable. Nevertheless, such action would have been of small moment had it not encouraged the capitalistic spirit for other reasons. We must hasten to add that such encouragement was unconscious on the part of the reformers. Of this we find proof in the fact that the theologians and moralists of the various sects opposed the manifestations of capitalism, in which they saw acts of Mammon. Bearing this in mind, we may extend to the whole of primitive Protestantism what Tawney wrote of its English forms : " If it is true that the Reformation released forces which were to act as a solvent of the traditional attitude of religious thought to social and economic issues, it did so without design, and against the intention of most reformers."[3] " We ought "—writes Weber—" to realize that the effects

---

[1] J. Wesley, *Works*, London, Wesleyan Conference Office, 1872, vol. XII, p. 455.
[2] W. J. Warner, op. cit., pp. 86–7.
[3] R. H. Tawney, *Religion and the Rise of Capitalism*, op. cit., p. 84.

of the Reformation on civilization were in great part "—
we ourselves should say for the most part—" consequences that the Reformers did not foresee, and indeed
definitely did not desire, and which often differed from
or conflicted with all that they hoped to obtain by their
ideals." [1]

Luther's conservatism in economic matters, to which
his patriarchal ideas on trade and his decided aversion
to interest [2] bear witness, has been proved beyond all
question. [3] Not only this, but there are writers who
definitely rule out that he could have brought " an urge
to enter the mighty progressive moment of modern
economic life." [4] Even Calvin, who when he seeks
social justification for commerce recalls St. Thomas, [5]
has violent attacks on Venice and Antwerp, which he
considers as centres of the Mammon of Catholicism.
With less precision than the Scholastics, but with an
equally anti-capitalistic bias, Calvin condemns as unlawful
all gain obtained at a neighbour's expense, and the
amassing of wealth " *pour remplir nostre avarice, ou
despendre en superfluité.*" [6] Nor does the Genevan
Reformer say anything that is new for Catholics when,

---

[1] M. Weber, *Die prot. Ethik*, op. cit., Chap. I.
[2] M. Luther, *Werke*, Erlangen, 1826–68, vol. XXII, p. 201, and vol. XXIII, p. 306.
[3] H. Grisar, *Luther*, Freiburg im Bresgau, Herder, 1912, vol. III, p. 579.
[4] E. Troeltsch, *Protestantism*, etc., op. cit. ; F. von Bezold, *Stato e Società nell'età della Riforma*, It. tr., Venice, " La nuova Italia," p. 120 ; M. Weber, op. cit., Chap. I.
[5] H. Hauser, *Les débuts*, etc., op. cit., p. 72. For Calvin's economic ethics, see E. Troeltsch, *Die Soziallehren*, etc., op. cit., pp. 705 et sq.
[6] J. Calvin, *Institution de la Religion Chrestienne*, Texte de la première édition française (1541), Paris, Champion, 1911, vol. I, p. 160.

speaking of the use of goods, he remarks that they must be used with moderation, since all that we possess is a deposit for which we shall have to render account.[1] If in regard to usury, for reasons that we shall see later, Calvin adopts a non-Catholic attitude, through the sixteenth and seventeenth centuries we find a continual repetition of the prohibitions of usury issued by the synods of the Huguenots and by those of the Dutch Reformers,[2] whose ethical code also condemned even excessive labour, as robbing time and energy from the service of God, and held action born of desire for gain to be a sign of madness.[3]

Nor did the Scottish Church show itself any more favourable to the first manifestations of capitalism.[4] The economic ethical code of the English Reformers and schismatics, in its most characteristic form, tends to agree with the most rigid Catholic view, and often goes even further. The ideas on property of the theologians of the Anglican Church in its early days derive from Scholastic doctrines.[5] We also find many echoes of these doctrines in the views of American Protestants of the eighteenth century.[6] The famous Bucer, in his *De Regno Christi*, starting from the gloomy statement that all traders are thieves, demands that only pious persons,

[1] J. Calvin, op. cit., vol. II, pp. 713–4 and 820–1.
[2] M. Weber, *Die prot. Ethik*, op. cit., Chap. II, art. 2.
[3] E. Beins, *Die Wirtschaftsethik der calvinistichen Kirche der Niederlande*, 1565–1650, Gravenhage, Nijoff, 1922.
[4] H. M. Robertson, op. cit., pp. 98–9.
[5] R. H. Tawney, op. cit., pp. 145–8.
[6] E. A. J. Johnson, *American Economic Thought in the Seventeenth Century*, London, King, 1932, pp. 84, 93–7.

more devoted to the State than to their own interests, should engage in commerce. Hipler goes further still, and in his *Divine Evangelical Reformation* demands the suppression of all merchant companies.[1] Wilson, in *A Discourse upon Usury* (1572), and Jewel, in his *Exposition upon the Epistle to the Thessalonians* (1583), support the English Protestant authorities who at the end of the eighteenth century still continue to forbid loans at interest.[2] On the other hand, Bullinger, author of the famous *Decadi*, follows Calvin in declaring such loans to be lawful. Anyone wishing to gain an idea of how a sixteenth-century Puritan regarded business has only to read Robert Crowley's verses on the merchant's behaviour in his *Voyce of the laste trumpet . . . calling al estats of men to the ryght path of their vocation*, published in 1550.[3]

[1] R. H. Tawney, op. cit., pp. 88 and 142. For Latimer's and Lever's opinions, see H. M. Robertson, op. cit., pp. 9–13.

[2] W. Ashley, *An Introduction to English Economic History and Theory*, London, Longmans, 1920–2, vol. II, p. 467. See also Tawney's fine preface to the 1925 edition of Wilson's work.

[3] Quoted by Robertson, op. cit., pp. 12–3.

> " Nowe marke my wordes thou marchaunte man
> Thow that dost use to bie and sell,
>   I wyll enstruct the, if I can,
> How thou maiste use thy callynge well.
>   Fyrst se thou cal to memori
> The ende wherfore al men are made,
>   And the endevour busily
> To the same ende to use thy trade.
>   The ende why all men be create,
> As men of wisdome do agre,
>   Is to maintaine the publike state
> In the contrei where thei shal be.
>   Apply thy trade therefore, I sai,
> To profit thy countrey with al ;
>   And let conscience be thy stay,
> That to pollinge thou do not fal. . . ."

The later-formed branches of the reformed religion showed themselves no less uncompromising. Various American Protestant sects pronounced in favour of a limitation of capitalistic industrialism.[1]

Among two sects, the Quakers and the Wesleyans, we find an alternation of rigid ordinances unfavourable to the expansion of economic life, with ordinances that seem to have facilitated the advent of capitalism.

The Quakers regulated even the details of the economic activity of their members, keeping watch that no one failed in respect of truth, in correct behaviour, in punctuality, and giving to each advice and financial assistance such as to enable him to succeed in business. It should be noted, however, that the motive for such facts does not seem to have been so much that of religion as the plain wish to gain friendship and toleration for the infant sect by good conduct in human relations. Once we have accepted this interpretation, which is favoured by the circumstances in which the Quakers had to work in the early years, good conduct in business will appear less a duty towards God than a means of apologetics. It was well to show that the Friends behaved with the utmost correctness, in order to gain new members. The same anxiety, though supported also by other motives, led to such an exaggeration—for so it appears from the purely religious point of view—as the exclusion of bankrupts from the sect.[2] Taken as a whole, this

---

[1] Todd, op. cit., pp. 568–88.
[2] I. Grubb, *Quakerism and Industry*, op. cit., pp. 90–2.

attitude undoubtedly helped to form the capitalistic
" type " among the Quakers, not so much through the
preaching of virtues—which were preached also by
Catholics—as by the emphasis on the economic virtues,
as though the exercise of these were the sole means of
giving glory to God.   Moreover, such preaching led to
a quest for good fame in the eyes of the world.   Thus,
instead of subordinating their works to extra-economic
laws, they subordinated them to success, sanctioning
the adoption of an intrinsic criterion of rationality.   On
the other hand, we must not forget that Quaker moral
teaching also contained rules that restricted the expansion
of economic activity.   Thus the prohibition of oath-
taking made it impossible for Quakers to belong to the
guilds.   The just-price theory maintained by Fox and
W. Smith (*Universal Love*, 1663) was opposed to speculation in wares.   The recommendation that Quakers
should help to maintain peace made it unfitting for them
to engage in war industries.[1]   A typical case of how
Quaker moral teaching could limit economic life is
provided by William Pegg.   He was a man with unusual
artistic gifts, and by their use was able to obtain very
well paid employment.   But, persuaded one day of the
necessity of obeying the commandment of Deuteronomy,
which the Quakers accept, to make no images, he gave
up his drawing, lost his post, and sacrificed his income.[2]
   The Wesleyans to a greater degree than the Quakers

----

[1] I. Grubb, op. cit., pp. 120, 130–1 and 134.
[2] I. Grubb, op. cit., pp. 106–7.

found an impulse to capitalistic action in their faith, which could well be reconciled with the necessities of a vigorous economic life.[1] Nevertheless, in John Wesley's moral teaching there are various restrictions that seem to conflict with the Methodist exhortation : " To gain all we can."   There is certainly nothing capitalistic in the rule that it was permissible to lend money at interest, but not beyond the legal rates.[2] Still less can we find a capitalistic spirit in Wesley's warning : " we cannot study to ruin our neighbour's trade in order to advance our own."[3]

Thus, on the whole, save for partial exceptions in the case of the Quakers and Wesleyans, the letter of Protestant moral teaching maintains a constantly critical attitude towards capitalism. This has led some to say that here Protestantism does not differ from Catholicism.[4] That Catholic teaching is reiterated by Protestants is indisputable ; we find that this is the case even in those expressions in Baxter, in which Weber has sought to find a departure from the Catholic attitude.[5] The demonstrable errors of this writer should make us very cautious in accepting views on the favour shown to capitalism by Protestantism, when they are based on a few moral maxims. Not seldom such convictions spring from the authors' ignorance of Catholic moral teaching.

[1] W. J. Warner, op. cit., p. 141.
[2] W. J. Warner, op. cit, p. 145.
[3] J. Wesley, *Works*, vol. VI, p. 128.
[4] H. M. Robertson, op. cit., pp. 6–7.
[5] A typical instance is where he forbids any waste of time (M. Weber, *Die prot. Ethik*, op. cit., Chap. II, art. 2).

They take for original sentiments what are often merely translations of Latin expressions of Catholic doctrine.[1]

Calvin, when he allows the lending of money at interest, is not reiterating Catholic social doctrine.[2] But this concession—which is an argument for the thesis of our next sub-section—by the very fact of the motives inspiring it, is contrary to Protestant praxis, which seeks a return to the doctrine of the Gospels. For its justification it depends on an idea of fundamental importance for our investigations—the uselessness of works as a means of salvation. Calvin no longer forbids usury, because he sees it as corresponding to the natural order of events, and in this sixteenth-century Calvinism is truly logical. If in judging other facts the Protestants adopted an attitude more akin to traditional teaching, it was because they did not draw the necessary consequences of their new basic principle, or else because they did not perceive the real nature of economic phenomena. Where it had this perception, and drew the logical conclusion, Protestantism was faithful to its " discovery " and showed itself in opposition to Catholic social ethics.

[1] We find no novelty in respect of Catholic moral teaching as expounded by Aquinas in the Wesleyan ideas that the subject may not defend his rights against the Government by forcible means; that the merchant must not injure his competitor by contracting for a different price than the market rate; that the rich man must not satisfy his needs in an immoderate degree (W. J. Warner, op. cit., pp. 110–1, 158). Moreover, the Wesleyan dictum, " The fault does not lie in the money but in them that use it " (J. Wesley, vol. VI, p. 126), which seems a great novelty to Warner (p. 138), is only an English rendering of St. Bernard's " *Argentum et aurum . . . nec bona sunt, nec mala : usus tamen horum bonus, abusio mala, sollicitudo pejor, quoesus turpior.*"

[2] For Calvin's theory of interest, see E. Böhm-Bawerk, *Kapital und Kapitalzins*, 4th ed., Jena, Fischer, 1921, vol. I, pp. 23–4.

A typical case is that of the Protestants of America, who at the beginning of the eighteenth century still observed rigid economico-ethical ideals, not unlike those of Catholicism, and who, as they became aware of the realities involved, ended by a practical indulgence, which, however, entailed no conflict with the fundamentals of their religion.[1]

Thus, when Robertson writes[2] that Protestantism did not influence capitalism, but capitalism influenced the social ethics of Protestantism, he is not saying anything new[3] nor anything absurd, though he should not find in this any cause for astonishment. For, once the idea was admitted that salvation was independent of works, with the idea of free enquiry, a Protestant was only acting in a logical manner if he accepted the rational order of the world as it resulted from the free operation of man. While the Protestant who still envisaged a "should-be" state was illogical. The fundamental principles of Protestantism lead inevitably to the sanctification of the real; the obstinate attempt to prescribe other-worldly limits to the world is a remnant of doctrines that Protestantism seeks to overthrow.

Weber's far-reaching hypothesis, with which he concludes his well-known study, on the possibility of the influence of social conditions on the development

---

[1] For example, it is among the Protestants of America, who began by demanding a rigorous moral control of commerce, that this control is relaxed after repeated experience of the benefits of individualism and freedom (E. Johnson, op. cit., Chap. VII, pp. 37 and 144–57).

[2] H. M. Robertson, op. cit., p. 32.

[3] L. Rougier, art. cit., p. 109.

of Protestant ethics, is ill-formulated inasmuch as it gives the idea of a deviating influence, whereas the course of events influenced Protestant ethics by making them ever more Protestant,[1] hence more logically consequent on the two fundamental principles of Protestantism than they were at first, when, though works were to receive no reward, they were still subject to an extrinsic law as though by that law they would be judged. It seemed at first as if the glory of God, not salvation, demanded an action in conformity with certain ideals. But as the idea of predestination developed, it was not hard to extend it to the circumstances, to the most trivial facts, of life, and this meant to free all action from any bonds not implied by its intrinsic rationality.

In final analysis, it is not on Protestant anti-capitalistic action[2] that we must base our estimation of the relationship between Protestantism and capitalism. It is the fundamental principle of Protestantism that counts; the limits set to economic life disappear as soon as a more penetrating logic deduces the full consequences of this principle.[3] The fabric of precepts is broken by

[1] With the passage of time, Protestantism lost what Catholic doctrine it had retained, side by side with its innovations in the early years of the revolt (G. O'Brien, *An Essay*, etc., op. cit., p. 31).

[2] Cunningham (*Christianity and Econ. Science*, op. cit., p. 58) holds that in any case such action was unable to check the progress of the commercial spirit, against which, when the authority of Rome was repudiated, there was no longer any power of adequate strength.

[3] Robertson, whom we have quoted several times, explains this successive adaptation by the predominance of human motives in the development of Protestantism. We cannot accept this explanation, but we hasten to add that this was inevitable and logical, given the initial Protestant separation of the human from the divine. It was logical and inevitable that economic rationality should establish itself in the economic world.

contact with life, which shows itself more orthodox than the moralists, and in the end leads even these to issue curious ordinances—like that of the Quakers, who expelled bankrupts from their sect[1]—through which religious motives became a spur to shrewd dealing; men were led to fear failure more as likely to entail excommunication than poverty.

3. According to Max Weber, Protestantism encouraged the development of capitalism by introducing into the world the idea of vocation, by which each individual was bound to devote all his powers to the field of work to which he was called, in the conviction that this was his sole duty towards God. In this we do not agree with Weber, although he is far more correct than those who declare that " compared with Catholicism, Protestantism in general perhaps gives greater encouragement to the spirit of individual initiative, since it confers on the individual direct and complete responsibility in the sight of God, and does not admit any intercession, neither that of the Saints, nor that provided by the prayers of others."[2] Leaving aside this utterly erroneous opinion,[3] we venture to say that

---

[1] I. Grubb, loc. cit.

[2] R. Michels, *Sunto di storia economica germanica*, Bari, Laterza, 1930, p. 25.

[3] Michels' mistake lies in the failure to remember that in Catholic doctrine the intercession of the Saints has nothing to do with individual responsibility. Such responsibility is in no doctrine so categorically asserted as in that of Catholicism, which relates salvation to works and faith, in contrast to the Protestants, who emancipate, so to speak, the individual from the weight of responsibility, making his salvation depend either on the immutable decrees of God, or on sole faith in the merits of the Redeemer.

Weber's solution is inacceptable for various reasons, above all because it does not admit that the capitalist spirit existed before the Protestant idea of vocation. It is true that Weber tries to anticipate the objection, that there were capitalistic manifestations prior to Protestantism, by attributing a different spirit to their authors and distinguishing between capitalism and the capitalist spirit,[1] but though his evasion of the objection is skilful, it altogether fails to satisfy. Is it possible for the essence of a thing—and for Weber the capitalist spirit constitutes the essence of capitalism—to come into existence long after the thing itself? We must none the less take Weber's theory into consideration if we are to understand the gravity of the true problem, which is quite other. And it is this: there were capitalistic "facts" before Protestantism, and if we admit that they could not be capitalistic unless they were produced by the capitalist spirit, we must conclude that the capitalist spirit existed before Protestantism. If we reason logically from the data with which Weber supplies us, we cannot fail to reach this conclusion. Therefore we cannot accept the idea of vocation as the origin of the capitalist spirit, or else we must say that it existed at an earlier date.

[1] M. Weber (*Die prot. Ethik*, op. cit., Chap. I, art. 3). He distinguishes the spirit of capitalism from capitalism, and declares that a capitalistic undertaking may be conducted in a "traditionalist" spirit. We quite understand that by capitalism Weber means an undertaking that is rationally organized from the technical standpoint, but we wonder what purpose is served by this confusion. We prefer to take our own distinction between technical forms and capitalism, understanding the latter as the system in which the capitalistic spirit dictates the rules of conduct.

On the other hand, we cannot grant that man never sought for gain in a rationalized manner before the idea of vocation. It is true that the idea of the rational is relative, but it is also true that the idea of the economically rational, the idea of the minimum means, though affected by later knowledge, was known before Protestantism. So much so, that at bottom those theorists are right who hold that, from the point of view of pure gain, and from the point of view of an economic rationality confined to scattered manifestations on the part of isolated individuals, capitalism has always existed. As against these, and against Weber, we would point out that man has an inborn instinct for gain; that he strives always to attain the minimum means as far as his state of knowledge allows; that external factors either check this instinct or encourage it. It is this instinct, this tendency, that is the germ of the capitalist spirit. Therefore, *in nuce*, the capitalist spirit has always been and always will be. But the capitalist spirit as a social force has not always been, nor will it always be. It is of this capitalist spirit that we speak and ought to speak. It is this that is the essence of capitalism as a social phenomenon; capitalism, so understood, has relations with the various religions, because these, in seeking to discipline the spiritual powers of man, can, in combination with other social phenomena, destroy it, check it, or stimulate it. They cannot bring it to birth, because it has been born already, or, rather, it is inborn in man.

But Weber's text lends itself to further criticism. A

few months ago Robertson proved that the idea of vocation, to which Weber attributes so great significance in determining the origin of the capitalist spirit, has not always implied what the German sociologist supposed. The Protestants of the sixteenth century, Latimer and Lever, for example, make use of the idea of vocation to combat those manifestations that Weber considers characteristic of the capitalist spirit.[1] Even in the seventeenth century the very Baxter whom Weber believes to supply so many proofs in support of his thesis attributes an ambiguous significance to the idea of vocation,[2] and only in the eighteenth century do we find among the Puritans a pro-capitalistic content to the idea of vocation.[3] The exhaustive proofs brought forward by Robertson, and which gain an added value from the conclusions of a work by Beins,[4] perhaps give him too great assurance, and he goes so far as to write that Weber's theory should be reversed and that the time has now come to ask whether it was not the predominance of a capitalist mentality in the middle classes that led to a slow but sure evolution of the social ethical code of Protestantism in a capitalistic sense. Robertson adds that no historian can be unaware that if the idea of vocation was the origin of capitalism, since this idea is identical in the Protestantism of the seventeenth century and the Catholicism of the fourteenth century, and in the

[1] H. M. Robertson, op. cit., pp. 9–13.
[2] Ibid., pp. 15–20.
[3] Ibid., pp. 25–8.
[4] E. Beins, op. cit.

Protestantism and in certain Catholic currents of the eighteenth century, we should have to conclude that Protestantism and Catholicism had an equal importance, in this respect, for the development of the capitalist spirit.[1] Nor does Robertson's observation appear ill-founded, once we realize that the idea of vocation, attributed by Weber to the Protestants, was a living idea before the Reformation, and remained alive in the Catholic camp even after. Bourdaloue, Houdry, Feugère, Griffet, Massillon, have repeatedly assured the faithful in France in modern times, not only that to each one God assigns a post in the world, but that it is God's will " *que chacun soit dans le monde parfaitement ce qu'il est*," [2] since " *accomplir fidèlement tous ses devoirs, . . . s'occuper de travailler, . . . agir dans son état selon la volonté et le gré de Dieu, c'est prier*," and that " *les devoirs d'état sont . . . en un sens de vrais devoirs de Religion* " [3] and " *l'état ou Dieu nous a placés* " is " *l'unique voie de notre salut*." [4] This most decidedly Catholic idea does not even lend itself to Groethuysen's [5] recent reproach that Catholic teaching condemned men's efforts to better their position, for, since Gaetano's sixteenth-century interpretation of St. Thomas' doctrine, it is plain that a man who seeks to obtain that position in life for which he is qualified by his gifts and capacities

[1] H. M. Robertson, op. cit., pp. 6–7, 30–1, 32.
[2] Bourdaloue, *Œuvres*, vol. II, p. 101.
[3] Griffet, *Sermons*, vol. II, p. 208.
[4] Massillon, *Petit carême, Sermon sur les Ecueils de la Piété des Grands*.
[5] B. Groethuysen, op. cit., pp. 284–5.

is not rebelling against God, but striving to reach the post that God has potentially assigned to him.

Weber's explanation is therefore inadequate, and we must ask whether there were not other ways in which Protestantism either encouraged or restrained the capitalist spirit—which has always existed in man in an embryonic state ; which, opposed and held in check by Catholicism, became a social force when, in the fifteenth century, Catholicism declined ; and which was encouraged by humanism inasmuch as humanism weakened Catholic ties.

Protestantism encouraged capitalism inasmuch as it denied the relation between earthly action and eternal recompense. From this point of view there is no real difference between the Lutheran and Calvinistic currents, for while it is true that Calvin linked salvation to arbitrary divine predestination, Luther made it depend on faith alone. Neither of the two connected it with works.[1] Nevertheless, Calvin's statement was the more vigorous, and therefore better able to bear practical fruit in a capitalistic sense.[2]

Such an assertion invalidates any supernatural morality, hence also the economic ethics of Catholicism, and opens the way to a thousand moral systems, all natural, all earthly, all based on principles inherent in

[1] For an exact analysis of the idea of predestination in the various Protestant denominations, there is nothing better than the second part of Weber's study.

[2] H. Grisar, op. cit., vol. II, pp. 158 et sq. ; E. Denifle, *Luther und Luthertum*, Mainz, 1904 (Fr. tr., Paris, 1910).

human affairs. Protestantism by this principle did not act in a positive sense, as Weber believes, but in a negative sense, paving the way for the positive action of innumerable impulses,[1] which—like the risks entailed by distant markets, in the pre-Reformation period, the price revolution at the time of the Reformation, and the industrial revolution in the period following—led man to direct his action by purely economic criteria. Catholicism acts in opposition to capitalism by seeking to restrain these impulses and to bring the various spheres of life into harmony on an ideal plane. Protestantism acted in favour of capitalism, for its religious teaching paved the way for it. Thus the effects of Protestantism combined with those of natural agencies, and Tawney's criticism of Weber does not apply.[2]

In the last chapter we saw how the capitalist spirit began by showing itself in the single act of a man who felt, momentarily, that he need not confine his activity within the limits prescribed by revealed morality. We saw, too, how a continuous series of such acts lessened

[1] Calvin had foreseen the consequence that we draw from his doctrine of salvation (op. cit., p. 402), and had objected that man will be led to perform good works not by the idea of reward, for such reward would be non-existent, but by the idea of saving the blood of Christ, which washes away sin. On p. 486 he reaffirms that the idea of predestination does not do away with anxiety to lead a good life, but on the contrary demands it. Anyone who thinks otherwise he dubs a " swine." Andrea Hyperius cannot have been of the same opinion, for he bears witness to the inadvisability of insisting so much on the doctrine that good works were not necessary, and fears the effects on manners (H. Grisar, op. cit., vol. II, p. 769). Indeed, the tone of morality in Protestant countries, according to witnesses contemporary with the Reformers, seems to have sunk in the first years after the Lutheran revolt (G. O'Brien, An Essay, op. cit., pp. 41 and 51–2).
[2] In his preface to the English translation of Weber's The Protestant Ethic, London, Allen & Unwin, 1930.

the possibility that they would be checked by remorse.[1] The possibility of remorse only disappears with the weakening of the conviction from which it springs. It is a case of separating the world from God, of unifying the duality of heaven and earth, so dear to the Christian ; of detaching earthly happiness from any higher destiny. This means to banish Saints and moralists, agonies and ecstacies.[2] Such was the work that humanistic scepticism began, and the positive teaching of Protestantism completed.[3] " The creation of a new mentality in the economic field cannot therefore be considered as the work of Protestantism, or rather of any one of the Protestant sects, but it is a manifestation of that general revolution of thought that characterizes the period of the Renaissance and the Reformation, by which in art, philosophy, religion, morals, and economy, the individual emancipates or tends to emancipate himself from the bonds imposed on him during the Middle Ages." [4] In this evolution Protestantism represents the stage at which religion perceives that business morality has legitimate foundations in the earth. If an action is to have no reward but its results, the rationalizing principle

[1] Groethuysen (op. cit., pp. 61–98) shows how the problem of death is connected with the bourgeois spirit, and how the bourgeois ended by abandoning the Christian conception of death as the hour of judgment.

[2] B. Groethuysen, op. cit., p. 163.

[3] Calvin establishes a clear separation between the divine and the human when he writes : " (Les) choses terriennes (doctrine politique, manière de bien gouverner sa maison, ars mecanicques, philosophie et toutes les disciplisnes qu'on appelle libérales) . . . ne touchent point jusques à Dieu et son Royaulme, ne à la vraye justice et immortalité de la vie future, mais sont conjoinctes avec la vie presente, et quasi encloses soubz les limites d'icelle " (J. Calvin, op. cit., vol. I, p. 54).

[4] G. Luzzatto, Storia econ., op. cit., p. 71.

of action will remain that of the maximum result. This is the profound revolution brought about by Protestantism, purely through the doctrines we have mentioned, and which acquire an immense significance inasmuch as they represent the religious beliefs of vast multitudes, for whom they become norms of life. Once human actions, including economic actions, must no longer be measured by the yard-stick of salvation, but by the yard-stick of success, man's struggle between his own instincts, his own needs, and divine commandment, finds a human solution. If God Himself allows intrinsic success to be the measure of order, and Himself guides man along this path,[1] does not the economic rationalization of economic actions become the realization of a divine plan? And does not the labour of the man who seeks to perform his task in the best manner possible— estimating the best manner solely from the point of view of results—become a tranquil labour, free from doubts, unhampered by uncertainty, unmarred by remorse?

By instilling this conviction into man, by basing human endeavours on this new rock, Protestantism favoured the dominance of the capitalist spirit, or, rather, it legitimized it and sanctified it. It transformed capitalistic efforts into religious efforts which, although not meritorious, for otherwise God would be rewarding man, were the sole way in which man could burn a grain of incense to the terrible Lord of Heaven and Earth.

[1] J. Calvin, op. cit., vol. I, pp. 90–1. Even in earthly dealings, God inspires man. More recent Protestant sects have still further accentuated the idea of continuous inspiration.

Truly Hauser is right when he declares: " Calvin, by boldly separating that which is God's from that which is man's, teaches that the Christian may attain salvation in his profession if he follows it as best he can and fully utilizes the gifts of God. . . . Calvin could not foresee a Rockefeller or a Carnegie. But nearer to Erasmus and Rabelais than he supposed, he helped to restore merely human virtue to its rights." [1] Thus Protestantism appeared as the religious sanction of the free efforts of man to attain wealth.[2] The capitalist spirit was justified and no opposition could be made to the action of those natural circumstances that urged man to arm himself to defend his economic interests to the last ditch.

In conclusion, Protestantism, as far as we are concerned, only marked a further stage in the emancipation of human action from supernatural limits. Working in this sense, it produced no new effects, but facilitated the manifestation of a movement that had shown perceptible signs of vitality before the Reformation, and which would continue its course after the Reformation, beyond what the Reformers intended, for, dreaming of a return to the Gospels, they never suspected what would be the fruits of their action.

4. Since the influence of Protestantism on the develop-

---

[1] H. Hauser, *La modernité*, op. cit., p. 50.

[2] It is well known that Marx (*Das Kapital*, Book I, Chap. XXVII) defined Protestantism as essentially a bourgeois religion. This expression was given more definite form when P. Lafargue (*L'origine ed evoluzione della proprietà*, Palermo, Sandron, 1896, p. 346) wrote that Protestantism is the true religious expression of the capitalistic form of production.

ment of modern capitalism appears thus limited, we are again faced by the problem which has been the source of all investigations into the relations between economic forms and religious forms: why was the development of capitalism more intense in Protestant than in Catholic countries? At one time it was believed that the solution of this problem was purely religious. It is indisputable that religion had its influence on this diversity of development. Not that it sowed the seeds, but inasmuch as it merely removed spiritual obstacles to a movement of which the *raisons d'être* are to be found in human instincts and in many factual circumstances.

It is an indisputable fact that the countries of North-Western Europe, from the sixteenth century onwards, economically outstripped the countries of the Mediterranean that had once been foremost. This, as we have shown, can be partly explained by religious differences, and partly by facts of a strictly economic nature that accompanied the Reformation, for instance, the confiscations. But the main explanation must lie with circumstances extraneous to the religious phenomenon. Assuredly not one of such circumstances by itself would explain the matter. Nor would all of them together have been able to lead to capitalism if the man facing them had had a hermit's ideals. But since they came about in a world in which man was led by instinct and reflection to seek the greatest possible gain, and when his way to such enrichment was no longer barred by religion, they appear as forces apt to produce that vast phenomenon in modern economics and society that we call the capitalist system.

For a long time the greater economic development of the countries of the North-West of Europe, from the sixteenth century onwards, was explained by the displacement of trade from the Mediterranean to the Atlantic, as a result of geographical discoveries and the difficulties of obtaining supplies in the markets of the Eastern Mediterranean, through the advent of the Turks. This explanation is not one to be set aside, although it is obvious that the effects of this were not immediate, and hence, if it holds good for the eighteenth century and after, it cannot be admitted for the sixteenth century, when, while the eastern coast of the Atlantic was rich in traffic, the western was still only half explored, and, since European-American trade on any large scale was almost the monopoly of Catholic Spain, could not offer any important source of trade to the English schismatics or the Dutch reformers.

What we might call the geographical explanation of capitalistic progress in North-West Europe seemed to be completed by Sombart's idea[1] that the reason for such progress was the displacement of the Jewish groups of Southern Europe towards the North. But this explanation is based on the hypothesis that Jewish moral teaching facilitates economic life, and this has not

[1] W. Sombart, *Die Juden und das Wirtschaftsleben*, Leipzig, Duncker-Humblot, 1911.

yet been fully proved.[1] Above all, it is based on the hypothesis that the Jews of Southern Europe, expelled in the sixteenth century, migrated to the North. " But in reality the great majority of such exiles migrated to the countries of the Ottoman Empire, and of the few tens of thousands received in the States of Western Europe only the small groups to which Antwerp and later Amsterdam gave hospitality enjoyed any wide freedom and could sometimes come to the fore in the greater commercial undertakings.[2]

Often those who have considered the problem of which we speak have forgotten certain essential points, namely, that if the capitalistic system is the system of mass production, its development can only come about where there is a huge market and a market rich in raw materials. Let them compare the Catholic countries from the fifteenth to the eighteenth century with the Protestant countries, and say whether by chance one of toe reasons for the more rapid economic development of the latter is not the fact that whereas Italy is economically divided into innumerable markets, the national State of England is already making giant strides towards unification,[3] of which it enjoys full benefit at a time when in Italy there are but a few individuals who dimly realize

---

[1] Cf. E. Crespi, *La morale commerciale nell'ebraismo*, Trieste, Lib. Minerva, 1934.

[2] G. Luzzatto, *Storia econ.*, op. cit., p. 70.

[3] From 1279 there was only one Mint in England (Chambers, *The London Mint*), and weights and measures were early made uniform. While England may be said to be the first country in Europe to achieve political unity, except for Scotland, even before the end of the Middle Ages.

the advantages to be derived from agreements between the various Italian States with a view to definite economic and political results.[1] The capitalistic importance of a vast and unified market—which is far greater than even the form of religion—can be seen by a summary comparison of the economic history of France and Germany. The former, Catholic and united, by the beginning of the nineteenth century has reached a pitch of economic development that the latter, Protestant and subdivided, does not dream of. And need we dwell on the fact that wealth of the raw materials indispensable to capitalistic industry helped to determine a greater capitalistic development of the Protestant countries? Could not France and Belgium, the only Catholic countries supplied with abundant coal and iron, sustain comparison with England[2] and the other Protestant capitalistic countries, as soon as abundance of coal and iron became indispensable to the development of industrialism?

Another reason that explains the different prosperity of the countries in question is the differing reserve of outlets. Italy, divided as she was during the Middle Ages, was queen of the European markets, and unrivalled

---

[1] A. Genovesi, " Digressioni economiche " in *Scrittori classici italiani di economia*, vol. X, Modern Section, p. 120. The real cause of Italian decadence, he remarks, "is that her own sons dismembered her into so many and such small sections that she lost her early name and her ancient vigour. This is a great cause of the ruin of nations. But none the less it would not have injured us so much if those many principalities, laying aside their needless jealousy . . . would give greater consideration to their own and common interests and come to some form of concord and unity."

[2] On p. 256, vol. I, of Nef's book he has a full analysis of the significance of the abundance of mineral coal in the capitalistic development of England.

in economic prosperity. Portugal, once small and feeble, became a great Power when she dominated the spice markets. But when, through various circumstances, England or Holland comes to enjoy a practical or legal monopoly in the non-European markets of the East or West, why should we forget this and seek other reasons for their prosperity ?

The unity of the market and its wide extension, both within and beyond national frontiers, is a factor beyond the compass of weak States, and the history of Europe in modern times shows us that in the Catholic countries we find weak or small States, which are therefore powerless to bridle, direct, and support the energies of their subjects. And when there was a strong and powerful State, it used its strength and power not for the achievement of better economic prospects, but frittered them away in political struggles. Spain is an example of this in one respect, and France in another. When Northern Europe saw the power of its States increasing, the States of Southern Europe were in decadence, or else, as in Italy, their development was arrested. Moreover, these Catholic States were dominated by aristocracies, while in the Protestant countries, whether kingdoms or republics, new bourgeois classes surrounded the Government, directing its policy in a mercantile sense. In earlier chapters we have shown how it is indispensable to capitalistic progress for the capitalistic classes to take their turn in government. Now, this came about earlier than elsewhere in Calvinistic Holland and in

214

Puritan England. Hence it is no wonder that the policy of these countries should have a definitely commercial trend, and that wars and peace might be said to have been determined solely by aims of expansion. Whereas in the plains of Europe and on the waters of the Mediterranean, in the intervals of the most tranquil court life imaginable, the peoples were often driven to the slaughter for the sake of some new, foreign king. Politics, in the strict sense, dominate the public life of the Southern European States. Economics, in the broad sense, direct the public life of the Northern European States. There is therefore no cause to wonder, and no need to seek for mysterious influences, if after three centuries of such life, in the nineteenth century, it becomes plain to all that the Nordic States are at the head of economic progress, while among those of the South there are a few trying to discover how to follow their example.

Each of these circumstances partially explains the phenomenon with which we are concerned. Taken together, combined with the encouragement brought to the capitalistic spirit by the Reformation, we think we have found a plausible explanation of the fact that from the sixteenth to the nineteenth century the Protestant countries are at the head of capitalistic progress, save in the case of Germany, which, politically divided, though Protestant, is only just beginning her advance, and France which, Catholic but united, rich in raw materials and in outlets, has many regions that, in respect of economic development, have no cause to envy the countries pointed out as models.

In concluding his preface to his collection of essays on the sociology of religions, Weber wrote of our problem as follows: "Finally, let us remember the anthropological aspect of these questions. If in apparently unrelated spheres we find the development of certain forms of rationalization to be confined to the West, the hypothesis naturally presents itself that they are the result of hereditary qualities. I admit that I am personally disposed to attribute great importance to biological heredity. But for the moment, in spite of the remarkable results of anthropological studies, I do not see any way to establish, even hypothetically, the measure and above all the mode and points of intersection of the influence of such heredity on the evolution that we are studying. It will be indeed one of the tasks of historical and sociological research to discover all the influences and those concatenations of causal connections that may find a satisfactory explanation in relations on events and on environment."

After reading this conclusion of Weber's preface, we may well ask whether we shall have to return to the racial explanation of the capitalistic phenomenon, advanced by Sombart,[1] and of which Leon Battista Alberti caught a glimpse,[2] or whether, rather, bearing in mind the recent tendencies of anthropometry, we

---

[1] Op. cit., on the Jews.
[2] L. B. Alberti, op. cit., p. 160.

should not make our research in this respect bear on physical constitution. When present studies on the relationship between constitution and character have led to more general conclusions, the future historian of capitalism will undoubtedly face the problem, asking if, by chance, in addition to the material and spiritual factors that to-day seem to explain the geographic localization of capitalistic manifestations, attention should not be paid to the different physical constitutions of the individuals in power. Or, since different peoples have successively found themselves at the head of capitalistic expansion, whether the diverse and alternate evolution of individual constitutions should not have a place in an explanation of the fact. We believe that in future research on our subject much attention will be paid to the fact that when the economic activity of the countries of Mediterranean Europe waned, it was at a period when dolichocephalic individuals came into power, as elements of the ruling classes. Whereas, the period of the revival of economic activity in the countries of Western Europe coincided with the advent of ruling classes prevalently composed of brachycephalic individuals.[1]

[1] See M. Boldrini, " Biotipi e classi sociali " in *Rivista Internazionale di Scienze Sociali*, 1932, pp. 3–28.

INDEX

224

THE EVOLUTION
OF CAPITALISM

Allen, Zachariah. **The Practical Tourist,** Or Sketches of the
State of the Useful Arts, and of Society, Scenery, &c.
&c. in Great-Britain, France and Holland. Providence,
R.I., 1832. Two volumes in one.

Bridge, James Howard. **The Inside History of the Carnegie
Steel Company:** A Romance of Millions. New York,
1903.

Brodrick, J[ames]. **The Economic Morals of the Jesuits:**
An Answer to Dr. H. M. Robertson. London, 1934.

Burlamaqui, J[ean-] J[acques]. **The Principles of Natural
and Politic Law.** Cambridge, Mass., 1807. Two volumes
in one.

Capitalism and Fascism: Three Right-Wing Tracts,
1937-1941. New York, 1972.

Corey, Lewis. **The Decline of American Capitalism.** New
York, 1934.

[Court, Pieter de la]. **The True Interest and Political
Maxims, of the Republic of Holland.** Written by that
Great Statesman and Patriot, John de Witt. To which
is prefixed, (never before printed) Historical Memoirs
of the Illustrious Brothers Cornelius and John de Witt,
by John Campbell. London, 1746.

Dos Passos, John R. **Commercial Trusts:** The Growth and
Rights of Aggregated Capital. An Argument Delivered
Before the Industrial Commission at Washington, D.C.,
December 12, 1899. New York, 1901.

Fanfani, Amintore. **Catholicism, Protestantism and
Capitalism.** London, 1935.

Gaskell, P[eter]. **The Manufacturing Population of England:** Its Moral, Social, and Physical Conditions, and the Changes Which Have Arisen From the Use of Steam Machinery; With an Examination of Infant Labour. London, 1833.

Göhre, Paul. **Three Months in a Workshop:** A Practical Study. London, 1895.

Greeley, Horace. **Essays Designed to Elucidate the Science of Political Economy,** While Serving to Explain and Defend the Policy of Protection to Home Industry, As a System of National Cooperation for the Elevation of Labor. Boston, 1870.

Grotius, Hugo. **The Freedom of the Seas,** Or, The Right Which Belongs to the Dutch to Take Part in the East Indian Trade. Translated with Revision of the Latin Text of 1633 by Ralph Van Deman Magoffin. New York, 1916.

Hadley, Arthur Twining. **Economics:** An Account of the Relations Between Private Property and Public Welfare. New York, 1896.

Knight, Charles. **Capital and Labour;** Including *The Results of Machinery.* London, 1845.

de Malynes, Gerrard. **Englands View, in the Unmasking of Two Paradoxes:** With a Replication unto the Answer of Maister John Bodine. London, 1603. New Introduction by Mark Silk.

Marquand, H. A. **The Dynamics of Industrial Combination.** London, 1931.

Mercantilist Views of Trade and Monopoly: Four Essays, 1645-1720. New York, 1972.

Morrison, C[harles]. **An Essay on the Relations Between Labour and Capital.** London, 1854.

Nicholson, J. Shield. **The Effects of Machinery on Wages.** London, 1892.

One Hundred Years' Progress of the United States: With an Appendix Entitled Marvels That Our Grandchildren Will See; or, One Hundred Years' Progress in the Future. By Eminent Literary Men, Who Have Made the Subjects on Which They Have Written Their Special Study. Hartford, Conn., 1870.

The Poetry of Industry: Two Literary Reactions to the Industrial Revolution, 1755/1757. New York, 1972.

Pre-Capitalist Economic Thought: Three Modern Interpretations. New York, 1972.

Promoting Prosperity: Two Eighteenth Century Tracts. New York, 1972.

Proudhon, P[ierre-] J[oseph]. **System of Economical Contradictions:** Or, The Philosophy of Misery. (Reprinted from *The Works of P. J. Proudhon*, Vol. IV, Part I.) Translated by Benj. R. Tucker. Boston, 1888.

Religious Attitudes Toward Usury: Two Early Polemics. New York, 1972.

Roscher, William. **Principles of Political Economy.** New York, 1878. Two volumes in one.

Scoville, Warren C. **Revolution in Glassmaking:** Entrepreneurship and Technological Change in the American Industry, 1880-1920. Cambridge, Mass., 1948.

Selden, John. **Of the Dominion, Or, Ownership of the Sea.** Written at First in Latin, and Entituled *Mare Clausum*. Translated by Marchamont Nedham. London, 1652.

Senior, Nassau W. **Industrial Efficiency and Social Economy.** Original Manuscript Arranged and Edited by S. Leon Levy. New York, 1928. Revised Preface by S. Leon Levy. Two volumes in one.

Spann, Othmar. **The History of Economics.** Translated from the 19th German Edition by Eden and Cedar Paul. New York, 1930.

The Usury Debate After Adam Smith: Two Nineteenth Century Essays. New York, 1972. New Introduction by Mark Silk.

The Usury Debate in the Seventeenth Century: Three Arguments. New York, 1972.

Varga, E[ugen]. **Twentieth Century Capitalism.** Translated from the Russian by George H. Hanna. Moscow, [1964].

Young, Arthur. **Arthur Young on Industry and Economics:** Being Excerpts from Arthur Young's Observations on the State of Manufactures and His Economic Opinions on Problems Related to Contemporary Industry in England. Arranged by Elizabeth Pinney Hunt. Bryn Mawr, Pa., 1926.